CAMP WOLTERS

MINERAL WELLS & WORLD WAR II

Stacy E. Croushorn

THE
History
PRESS

Published by The History Press
Charleston, SC
www.historypress.com

Front cover, top: The first troops that arrived at Wolters were African Americans from Oklahoma. *Courtesy* Fort Worth Star-Telegram, *March 1941, Special Collections, University of Texas at Arlington Libraries*; bottom: Army Day at Camp Wolters, April 7, 1941. *Courtesy* Fort Worth Star Telegram Collection, Special Collections, University of Texas at Arlington Libraries.
Back cover, top: Camp Wolters mail. *Courtesy* Fort Worth Star-Telegram, *December 17, 1944, Special Collections, University of Texas at Arlington*; middle: Camp Wolters Orchestra. *Courtesy* Fort Worth Star-Telegram, *June 6, 1941, Special Collections, University of Texas at Arlington*; bottom: Judy Garland visiting Camp Wolters. *Courtesy* Fort Worth Star-Telegram, *January 30, 1942, Special Collections, University of Texas at Arlington*.

First published 2023

ISBN 9781540257086

Library of Congress Control Number: 2022951593

Notice: The information in this book is true and complete to the best of our knowledge. It is offered without guarantee on the part of the author or The History Press. The author and The History Press disclaim all liability in connection with the use of this book.

For my beloved parents, Captain George A. Croushorn, USAF, and June Shewmake Croushorn.

CONTENTS

ACKNOWLEDGEMENTS

T his book is a condensed version of the thesis I wrote for the master's program in history at the University of Texas at Arlington. Research was conducted during COVID-19 shutdowns, and I was unable to gain access to several archival collections that would have been very useful to this book. I wish to recognize the following people who played a decisive role in the creation of this book and thesis: James Teel, Gwinnetta Crowell, Charles and Betty Shewmake, Dr. Gerald Saxon, Dr. Stephanie Cole and Dr. James Sandy. Thank you for your time and assistance.

INTRODUCTION

On September 16, 1940, the Burke-Wadsworth Act passed both houses of Congress and became Public Law 76-783, also known as the Selective Service Act, or the draft. In Section 3, Subsection A, the law provides for the shelter and welfare of all selectees being trained for military service. Millions of American citizens, both men and women, served their country during World War II and had to be trained for a wide variety of work. This led to training facilities being built across the country and was a boon to many local economies. This book focuses on one of the many training facilities and the relationship it had with the neighboring town.

Camp Wolters was an Infantry Replacement Training Center (IRTC) three miles east of Mineral Wells, Texas, during World War II and had a great impact on the town of Mineral Wells and the residents of Palo Pinto County. This book explores the growth of Mineral Wells while Camp Wolters was open, 1941–46, and attempts to bring understanding to this boom time.

Texas was home to 142 military installations during World War II, and all left their mark on the surrounding towns and areas in which they were located.[1] There have been studies of military installations across the South but very few in Texas and none on the IRTCs. Historians have written about the impact of the military in relation to the South and Southwest in general and have made clear that the military changed the face and future of whatever area in which they chose to locate an encampment. Only one detailed study of a Texas installation and its economic impact on the city in which it was located is known to exist.[2] Much more work needs to be done on the history of the military in Texas during World War II. Each of the 142 military installations has a story, a story that involves more than learning drills and how to shoot a BAR gun. These stories involve the people, communities and businesses that made the military want to come to that town, that made life a little happier for the selectees and that forever changed the citizens of that community.

While Mineral Wells always had welcomed visitors, the relaxed pace its citizens were used to quickly became a memory as thousands of workers and then thousands of soldiers came swarming into this drowsy little city at the end of 1940. In mere months, the population tripled; the water, sewage and school systems were pushed to maximum capacity; and the police department, fire department and sheriff's office were plagued with all types of problems resulting from such a huge influx of people in such a short time. However, banks celebrated as the biggest payroll in Texas was heading their way. By the end of the World War II era (roughly 1946–50), the population for Mineral Wells had increased 8.3 percent, the yearly income for Palo Pinto County had increased 78.3 percent and county retail sales receipts had increased 64 percent.[3] With this monetary increase came a 59.8 percent increase in new home sales, an updated and improved septic and water system, improved community centers and recreational facilities and an expanded school system.[4] Not only did Camp Wolters help win World War II, but it also paved a bold and bright future for the "Town Built on Water."[5]

Chapter 1

BACKGROUND OF MINERAL WELLS

After the passage of the Defense Act of 1920 and an increased budget, the U.S. Army sought locations to build training facilities and transform the diverse sections of the army into a united militia. Mineral Wells, long known as a resort and convention town, attracted the attention of the Texas National Guard (the Guard). Mineral Wells offered a variety of amusements and was easily accessible. After Mineral Wells became home to the Guard's summer encampment, the town was considered for a permanent Guard facility. This laid the path for future military involvement.

After World War I, military leaders in the United States realized there needed to be more coordination among the different parts of the army;, specifically, the training programs needed improvement and modernization. At this time, the army consisted of three sections: the regular or professional army, the National Guard and the Organized Reserves. After military leaders discussed what needed to be changed within their organizations, they spoke with political leaders to pass legislation that could bring about these changes. The Defense Act of 1920, which increased the number of men in the armed forces, attempted to bring the training of the different army groups into line with each other and required planning for mobilization in the event of another war.[6] With this increased effort came federal money for training camps, uniforms and supplies for all sections of the army. This resulted in the establishment of multiple National Guard training camps around the country, including Camp Wolters in Mineral Wells, Texas, which became the summer training camp for the Guard.

The Weatherford, Mineral Wells and Northwestern train at the Mineral Wells Depot, 1899. *Courtesy A.F. Weaver Collection, Boyce Ditto Library, Special Collections.*

The Guard had already established an infantry company and an armory at Mineral Wells in 1915.[7] When federal money became available, the Guard decided to establish and expand permanent training facilities and began looking for appropriate training areas. With the armory already in Mineral Wells, it was logical that the town wanted to become home to a larger, more permanent facility that could make a favorable economic impact. Just holding the annual summer encampment of the Guard gave a city an opportunity to earn some of the $300,000 in pay and subsistence monies allocated for this training.[8]

Mineral Wells had many features that benefitted the Guard. It was easily accessible by train, as the Weatherford, Mineral Wells and Northwestern Railroad opened in 1891 and had a large depot.[9] The T&P (Texas and Pacific Railway) bought out the line in 1902.[10] The motorcar was welcome in Mineral Wells, as it became the midpoint on the Bankhead Highway, the nation's first highway that stretched coast to coast.[11] Mineral Wells was well known as a "spa resort town" and had multiple amenities that had been welcoming visitors for decades.[12] Before the town was incorporated, the mineral waters of Mineral Wells had been drawing crowds of health seekers looking to improve their physical and mental well-being.[13]

Mineral Wells was the quintessential resort town when the Guard was considering locations for a permanent facility. Janet Mace Valenza refers to this period (1890–1919) as the "Golden Age" of health resorts in Texas, with Mineral Wells being one of the largest spa resort towns during this time.[14] She notes that for a town of roughly 8,000 people, Mineral Wells had over 150,000 visitors a year.[15] She continues that Mineral Wells "became the model for new resort towns."[16] People came to Mineral Wells for the health benefits but also to be entertained. Mineral Wells offered all sorts of attractions. There were donkey rides going up East Mountain, hiking trips, motor car scenic tours, bowling alleys, nickelodeons, swimming pools, manicured gardens, saloons, barber and hair salons, playgrounds for the children, multiple bandstands and an amusement park, Elmurst Park. Elmhurst Park stretched over one hundred acres, had its own lake with boats to rent, multiple cafés, dancing pavilions, bandstands, "high-class vaudeville" entertainment, a skating arena, a merry-go-round and a 1,500-seat casino.[17] In 1920, Mineral Wells had earned the moniker the "South's Greatest Health Resort."[18] Many well-known entertainers, celebrities and athletes came to Mineral Wells for a rest or for the health benefits, including D.W. Griffith, Will Rogers, Spanky McFarland, Minnie Pearl and General John J. Pershing, and the town became a training camp to the Chicago White Sox, Philadelphia Phillies, Cincinnati Reds, St. Paul Saints, Dallas Steers, Fort Worth Cats, the House of David baseball teams and the St. Louis Browns.[19] Numerous organizations held their annual conventions in Mineral Wells. Winnie McAnelly Fiedler states that "twenty to thirty major organizations" held their annual conventions there.[20] Among these organizations were the Texas Medical Association, both the state Republican and Democratic Conventions, the General Baptist Convention of Texas, the Texas Bar Association and the Texas Chamber of Commerce.[21] What this meant was that Mineral Wells was no stranger to having thousands of visitors and showing them a good time.

The Casino at Elmhurst Park. *Courtesy A.F. Weaver Collection, Boyce Ditto Library, Special Collections.*

Another fact, or rather another person, in favor of Mineral Wells was W.P. (Bill) Cameron. Cameron was a supply officer in the 112th Cavalry, but his day job was being business manager for the *Mineral Wells Index*, one of the town's newspapers. He was also a good friend of General Jacob Wolters, commander of the 56th Cavalry Brigade of the Guard, who decided where the cavalry would be permanently housed and would spend the summer training.[22] Mineral Wells made a good case for its selection, and General Wolters made his announcement on January 15, 1927, that Mineral Wells was his choice as a home for the cavalry.[23] Fiedler states that "Cameron was instrumental" in getting Wolters to settle on Mineral Wells.[24] On February 24, 1927, the state accepted fifty acres near Mineral Wells in Palo Pinto County and expressed its gratitude in writing to the Mineral Wells Chamber of Commerce and the donors of the property.[25]

The federal government allocated $25,000 for the new encampment.[26] This included construction of fourteen mess halls, five bath houses, sixteen latrines, a water and sewage system and a supply building.[27] The state paid $1,100 for a storage building at the site.[28] Facilities were ready by July 10, 1927, when the Guard received fifty carloads of horses for use during the summer training session.[29] By July 22, all troops had arrived and paraded in front of the governor and other representatives for official review.[30] Summer training lasted two weeks and was held every July until the beginning of World War II.

The camp was named after the commander of the Fifty-Sixth Cavalry, Jacob Wolters. He was an enigmatic figure who led the cavalry on some of its most harrowing missions.[31] Wolters joined the Guard as a private in 1891 and retired as a breveted major general in 1934. He is considered the "Father of the present Texas Cavalry."[32]

The Civilian Conservation Corps (CCC) Company No. 1811 came to Camp Wolters on June 17, 1933, and stayed until January 2, 1934.[33] It improved much of the camp, including covering the buildings with a rock veneer, constructing mess halls, barracks and warehouses.[34] The Works Progress Administration (WPA) allotted $33,958 for improvement to the camp from 1937 to 1938.[35] It built additional stables, laid rock sidewalks, made stone fences and constructed an entrance gateway.

Because of tensions in Europe, on August 31, 1940, President Franklin Delano Roosevelt (FDR) issued Executive Order 8530, which activated the National Guard for twelve months.[36] The Guard reported for duty on September 16, 1940, and began mobilizing and training for war. The Guard stationed at Camp Wolters participated in the Louisiana Maneuvers,

The entrance to Camp Wolters built by the CCC in the 1930s. *Courtesy A.F. Weaver Collection, Boyce Ditto Library, Special Collections.*

a massive undertaking of molding 400,000 men into a coordinated, united, mobile army.[37] These maneuvers allowed the army to gauge the caliber and effectiveness of training on the first soldiers who would hit the ground in the event of war and revise training plans for any new recruits who entered the army after this point. There would be millions of men in need of training very soon.

The Defense Act of 1920 enabled the Guard to train, supply and build permanent military facilities. When General Wolters chose Mineral Wells as the permanent location for the Fifty-Sixth Cavalry, Mineral Wells leaders enthusiastically embraced this opportunity to promote the town and make the town's attractions known to a wider population. By the late 1930s, the spa resort industry was in decline, and Mineral Wells needed something to fill the economic void. While the Great Depression wiped out whatever financial gains were made during this time, having the Guard camp added to Mineral Wells' appeal as a military town.[38] It also helped the town lure a much bigger fish to its little pond in the next decade, the United States Army.

Chapter 2

WAR COMES TO A SMALL TOWN

T ension ran high around the world as the 1930s ended. Two continents were already at war, and the possibility of bringing others into the fray was increasing. U.S. leaders had to prepare the nation for a war that they did not want but would become drawn into. Military leaders made plans to train and supply the army, while the U.S. president supported and helped pass the first ever peacetime draft. Millions of men needed to be ready if, or when, war came, and they had to have the facilities and equipment necessary for training and fighting. The U.S. economy boomed with contracts for supplying the military. Cities would try to lure military training bases, worth millions of dollars, to their local economy. The city of Mineral Wells, Texas, was one of numerous cities that wanted an army base, and it ended up getting the largest Infantry Replacement Training Center (IRTC) in the country, based at Camp Wolters. The army poured money into Camp Wolters getting it ready to train thousands of men. An army of workers had to transform the rocky, cedar-lined hillsides into level ground for the building of a camp capable of housing seventeen thousand soldiers. The construction effort was momentous and difficult. With days of endless rain and knee-deep mud, markets and restaurants running out of food and people sleeping in shifts in the same bed, Mineral Wells experienced a time of extremes. However, it was well worth the effort as Mineral Wells became a rapidly growing military town.

Most Americans had hopes that the new decade of the 1940s would be much better than the previous ten years. The 1930s had been a rough, agonizing period of loss, fear and struggle for the American people. The decade ended on a more positive note with unemployment dropping and the demand for goods increasing as the United States began exporting more products to a war-torn Europe.[39] The 1930s had ended with two active wars, one in Europe and the other in Asia (the Second Sino-Japanese War). The United States was trying desperately to stay out of both conflicts. As the new year progressed and the Allies struggled, the ability of the United States to remain neutral became questionable. Government and military officials knew that the country had to be prepared.

In January 1940, FDR submitted the annual budget to Congress with a $1.8 billion increase for national defense.[40] Making his case for this increase, FDR said, "Even as...we prepare to cooperate in a world that wants peace, we must likewise be prepared to take care of ourselves if the world cannot attain peace."[41] FDR had sent Germany's leader, Adolf Hitler, a letter asking for peaceful negotiations between European parties before the outbreak of war.[42] Hitler had responded, "The possibilities of arriving at a just settlement by agreement are therefore exhausted."[43] FDR knew war was coming, and he had to prepare the nation. As the war in Europe continued to ramp up, FDR asked Congress for an additional $1 billion for defense in May.[44] In August, FDR activated the National Guard and Reserves,[45] and there was much discussion about the passage of the Burke-Wadsworth Act (Selective Service or draft).[46] The act represented, for the first time in American history, a potential military draft executed before a declaration of war. Passed on September 16, the new law required all able-bodied men, between the ages of eighteen and thirty-six, to register for possible induction into the military for a twelve-month period. The first round of trainees was selected on October 29; they had until November 18 to prepare to leave for training.

The legislation also had implications for Mineral Wells and other cities across the nation. Among the multiple provisions was Section 3(a), which stated,

That no men shall be inducted for such training and service until adequate provision shall have been made for such shelter, sanitary facilities, water supplies, heating and lighting arrangements[,] medical care, and hospital accommodations, for such men as may be determined by the Secretary of War and the Secretary of Navy, as the case may be, to be essential to public and personal health.[47]

This one sentence caused a flurry of economic, martial and social upheaval. The requirement was welcomed by myriad businesses that would benefit from this act. Commercial and defense manufacturers were pushed to limits that had been previously thought unobtainable. The impossible became possible as the public gave the new soldiers its total support. Training and housing an expanded military employed thousands of workers, men and women, across the nation, presaging the rearmament that also rebuilt the economy and brought a glimpse of economic hope.

The military needed numerous camps and training centers to be erected and activated to house and train these men. Not everyone looked favorably on passage of the draft, but there were men, businessmen particularly, who were anticipating this moment and were ready to jump at this economic opportunity once the act passed Congress. The fact was that many states, towns and businesses were betting their financial livelihoods on passage of this act, as the stronghold of the Great Depression was still being felt across the country. Securing a government contract enabled a business or city to put the vestige of the Great Depression in their rearview mirror and focus on a brighter, more secure future.

The passage of the draft did not come as a surprise to the many defense-oriented businesses or municipalities that stood to benefit. City leaders of Mineral Wells had been discussing how to lure an army camp to the city since May. This small town of 6,303 people held a national reputation for being a popular resort spot that could accommodate 5,000 at a time and annually welcomed over 200,000 visitors.[48] The town boasted two luxury hotels: the Crazy Water Hotel and the Baker Hotel. A new Crazy Water Hotel opened on March 11, 1927, at a cost of $1 million.[49] The original Crazy Water Hotel had burned in 1925. The Baker Hotel opened on November 20, 1929, just weeks after the economic collapse of Wall Street, and cost $1.2 million. It is the tallest structure in Mineral Wells, standing fourteen stories high, and has four hundred rooms.[50] Both hotels have welcomed numerous celebrity guests, including Judy Garland, Clark Gable, Marlene Dietrich, the Three Stooges, Bonnie and Clyde, Lyndon Johnson, Jim Wright, Sam Rayburn, Ronald Reagan, Mary Martin and many others.[51]

Along with an entertainment infrastructure, the presence of the Guard encampment of Camp Wolters, located just a few miles east of the city, was in the town's favor. Local businessman Fred Brown was credited with coming up with the idea that Mineral Wells would be a perfect location for an army camp and brought the idea up during a session of the Mineral Wells Chamber of Commerce (CoC).[52] There, the topic took on new

The Baker Hotel, 1948. *Courtesy* Fort Worth Star-Telegram *Collection, October 1940, Special Collections, University of Texas at Arlington Libraries.*

life, other members rallied behind the proposal, and the CoC officially endorsed the idea. It formed committees and laid out plans to hook an army camp.

The CoC committee began busily writing letters, visiting officials, photographing the area and preparing briefs that showed the advantages of having an army center located in Mineral Wells. The committee members asked officials to visit and see for themselves why the town was a perfect fit for an army base. As commanding general of the Eighth Corps Area, Lieutenant General Herbert J. Brees made the decision as to which cities made the final list of potential army centers. His staff visited Mineral Wells during the summer of 1940.[53] On August 31, a letter arrived at the headquarters for the commanding general of Area 8 (Fort Sam Houston) requesting

Top: Fred Brown is credited with the idea of bringing an army camp to Mineral Wells. *Courtesy* U.S. Army Speedometer, *1941, Boyce Ditto Collection, Special Collections.*

Bottom: Photograph of Morris Sheppard, U.S. senator from Texas, 1913–41. He was chairman of the Senate Committee on Military Affairs. *Courtesy United States Library of Congress.*

that Major General Walter Kreuger investigate the possibility of leasing land adjacent to Camp Wolters on behalf of the army.[54] Mineral Wells had made the list of possible locations! The town was in the running! Excitement coursed through the city. The city and CoC had a long list of things they needed to do before they could be selected, but everyone was confident that Mineral Wells would get a camp. On a side note, it was beneficial that the president of the CoC, H.A. (Allen) Guinn (district manager of Texas Power and Light) was married to the niece of Jesse H. Jones,[55] the newly appointed U.S. secretary of commerce. Also, the chairman of the Senate Committee on Military Affairs, Morris Sheppard, had recently had a new multimillion-dollar dam named after him in the county in which Mineral Wells was located.[56]

The CoC quickly formed two committees to work on the final stages of getting the camp: (1) the Steering Committee (headed by Irl Preston, president of City National Bank) and (2) the Land Committee (headed by E.L. Malsby, of Malsby Dairy). Other members of the committees were H.H. Collins, E.J. Benavides (vice-president and managing director of the Baker Hotel), John Tom Bowman and B.A. Yeager (president of the Mineral Wells State Bank) (Steering Committee) and F.C. Myers (local car dealer), W.M. Woodall, Fred Brown (assistant manager of the Baker Hotel), R.L. Bowden (Bowden's Department Store), O.H. Grantham (local insurance agent), George Ritchie (attorney), W.O. Gross (attorney) and H.E. Dennis (general manager of Turner-Wagley Motor Company) (Land Committee). A third committee, the Military Finance Committee, chaired by H.E. Dennis, was formed to address the cost of the camp to the city.[57] Citizens of Mineral Wells and Palo Pinto County wholeheartedly supported this endeavor. The CoC publicly thanked several private citizens, including John Davidson (Davidson Hardware), W.P. Cameron (*Mineral Wells Index*), C.B. Baughn and Mineral Wells mayor John Miller for their efforts in acquiring the camp.[58] By September 13, the county newspaper, the *Palo Pinto County Star*, was reporting that Mineral Wells would probably receive "the big camp."[59] Land was scouted and deeds researched, and chamber members began visiting every rancher and farmer who owned land in the Camp Wolters area. On September 27, Mr. and Mrs. Allen Guinn and Fred Brown flew to Washington, D.C., to discuss the committee's progress with military planners.[60]

While the CoC continued its search for land, it also began looking for money to purchase that land, as the War Department had asked for financing.[61] The CoC committees came together and requested a meeting with the mayor of Mineral Wells, John Miller, and city commissioners. Knowing that acquisition of the camp would lead to a huge increase in economic activity (the soldiers had a monthly payroll of $600,000)[62] the city voted to purchase the appropriate land and lease it to the army.[63] In the meantime, the city had to expand all its public utilities. Mineral Wells installed a new water facility that could deliver the 1.5 million gallons of water that the camp required daily.[64] Additional police and emergency services were added, streets widened and repaved, permits issued and new housing erected for military families, and all sorts of commercial enterprises were encouraged (cafés, various types of stores, entertainment facilities, etc.). This was an undertaking unlike anything the city, or county, had ever seen before.

The CoC successfully leased 7,300 acres of land from multiple farmers and ranchers and assured the army that additional land would be available if needed. The land came mostly from three sources: the Loveless tract, which was part of the defunct town of Rock Creek; the Beetham land; and the Howard property that was by Lake Mineral Wells.[65] The additional land they found was needed; by the end of World War II, the army leased slightly over 16,000 acres from the city (part of this land included the ROTC site Camp Dallas).[66] A "master lease" was offered to the army at the prescribed $1 per acre required by the army.[67] The army issued a check to the City of Mineral Wells for $7,300 renewable yearly.

The official announcement came on October 13 that Mineral Wells had been selected for an army camp. The army required all facilities be ready by March 1, 1941. The camp would have the capacity to train 17,000 men at once, and the first construction quartermaster was Major E.S. Armstrong. Mineral Wells was not going to get just any army camp; this camp was the largest IRTC in the entire nation.[68] Mineral Wells residents were "exuberant" at the news.[69] The War Department appointed General A.G. Kanalser, of Fort Sam Houston, as their leasing agent. It was estimated that the camp would take four months to build and cost between $3 and

F.T. Maddux sold land for the building of Camp Wolter. *Courtesy* Fort Worth Star-Telegram *Collection, October 1940, Special Collections, University of Texas at Arlington Libraries.*

$7 million (this amount would double before completion). It was estimated that maintenance costs of the camp would run around $500,000 a month. Troops were scheduled to arrive on March 15, 1941; there would be 15,000 white troops and "2,000 Negroes."[70] Leases were officially signed on October 24 at Fort Sam Houston, with Colonel John P. Hasson signing for the army and Mayor John C. Miller signing for the city, along with Mineral Wells representatives Owen Boarman, Allen Guinn, W.O. Gross, Paul Ord and C.P. Scudder attending.[71]

Mineral Wells lost no time beginning preparations, as the next day the Palo Pinto County Commissioners Court called an emergency meeting. The commissioners declared that having the army camp located in the county, on unincorporated land, had caused an emergency situation, and they responded to this situation by creating the Sanitary District of the "Unincorporated Town of Greater Mineral Wells."[72] The commissioners appointed Dr. Edward Yeagar, Dr. J.E. St. Clair and Frank Myers to head this new district and told them they were to work closely with all the different parties to make sure that "a consistent and uniform program be carried out and established" for the disposal of waste from this area.[73]

Left to right: E.J. Benavides, Major E.S. Armstrong, John Miller and Allen Guinn. *Courtesy Fort Worth Star Telegram Collection, November 12, 1940, Special Collections, University of Texas at Arlington Libraries.*

The court also asked contractors to use local laborers first when filling jobs. Harold Reinhart of the Texas Employment Services in Mineral Wells began registering potential employees as soon as the official announcement was issued. Texas Power and Light and the T&P Railway also started hiring new employees.

On November 4, one hundred engineers from the company of Rollins and Forrest began surveying and mapping out the boundaries of the camp. They were treated to an appreciation dinner at the Baker Hotel the next evening sponsored by the Junior Chamber of Commerce.[74] People started swarming into the town. Citizens began renting out rooms as hotels quickly filled up. Oscar Rankin, tax assessor for the county, said business had picked up, people were paying their back taxes, and he was receiving all kinds of questions about taxes from people.[75] The Railroad Commission received an application for a new bus line to run from Mineral Wells to Camp Wolters from Fort Worth businessman Rudy Copeland.[76] Colonel C.H. McCall purchased part of the Lawn Terrace and Highland Park additions in the Southwest part of the city, where he intended on improving the area and selling to new homeowners.[77]

This photo shows laborers (*left*) laying tar paper. *Courtesy* Fort Worth Star-Telegram *Collection, January 2, 1941, University of Texas at Arlington Libraries.*

Construction contracts were awarded on November 8 to Cage Brothers and F.M. Reeves and Sons. The camp was to be three times the size of the city and span two counties, Palo Pinto and Parker.[78] They estimated they would need between 7,500 and 10,000 workers to complete the project on time, with a price of $6,045,000.[79] The price tag would include: "280 barracks, 6 barracks for medical personnel, a laundry, bakery, mess halls, headquarters, recreation halls, classrooms, incinerators, cold storage plant, a hospital and quarters, utilities building, etc. approximately 600 or more buildings in all."[80] Actual work began on November 16.[81]

Along with the need to build the camp quickly, the town faced a number of problems connected with the rapid population growth. Mineral Wells mayor John C. Miller said that the three most pressing problems were "traffic congestion, sanitation, and housing."[82] The population of Mineral Wells was 6,303 in 1940; the county population was 18,456.[83] Four months later, the population of Mineral Wells would reach 25,000.[84] The sudden influx of people caused immense problems for this small town. All hotels and boardinghouses were full, homeowners were renting out rooms, barns were transformed into additional boardinghouses, people were sleeping in their cars and "mushroom accommodations" were springing up on every parcel of land.[85] People even altered their tile chicken houses into sleeping quarters.[86] Rents skyrocketed.[87] Store owners ran out of inventory as soon as they put it on the shelves. Banks tripled their staffs. The post office was overwhelmed by the additional business from camp workers. Previously, the post office processed 100 money orders on a busy day, but when construction began, it processed an average of 381 per day.[88] It had been sending out around 25 parcels a day; that number quickly became 116.[89] The post office turned the basement of its building into a post office for the camp and hired an additional fifteen people. The cafés and "food joints" were often sold out, and many had to close before dinner.[90] Merchants were working seventeen to eighteen hours per day trying to keep up with demand and trying to protect their stores from being robbed.[91] City officials complained about the increase in "police problems, traffic problems, health and sanitation problems, together with housing problems, fire and merchandizing problems,"[92] all confronting the city at an alarming rate. The Mineral Wells police department added more policemen, bringing the police force to nine, and the sheriff's department added two new deputy sheriffs.[93]

An example of short-term dwellings made by workers from the camp. *Courtesy* Fort Worth Star-Telegram *Collection, December 1940, Special Collections, University of Texas at Arlington Library.*

With a larger population came a number of issues. Fires were a constant problem; one example is the nighttime fire at the Lake Charles Hotel on December 10 that resulted in numerous workers losing everything they owned.[94] The yearly flu bug hit big that year too, and the Red Cross put out an urgent call for nine hundred nurses needed at all army posts. Even though the camp hospital had not yet opened, the Red Cross advertised for one hundred nurses at Camp Wolters.[95] Things were getting a bit out of hand during these boom times, but good things were happening too. It was reported that sales receipts had tripled, new permanent home construction had begun and bank deposits were up $1.5 million.[96] The new bus line opened that ran from Mineral Wells to the camp, called the Army Camp Bus Line, and ran four brand-new buses.[97] The first couple from Camp Wolters to be married were Miss Freida Hight from the quartermaster's staff and Pitt Milner of Dallas.[98] They married at the First Methodist parsonage on December 20; three more couples would take the plunge by February 7, 1941.[99]

Problems were not isolated to just the city; there were problems at the camp, too, but of the kind that nobody could do anything about. It rained consistently for thirty days. Of the four months that construction crews had to work, only two and a half of those months were workable.[100] From the start of construction in November until January 14, 1941, it rained 62 percent of the time.[101] According to the U.S. Weather Bureau, Mineral Wells received 4.78 inches of rain that November. That was the most rain in the month of November for twenty years.[102] Construction continued during the rain, but the rain caused multiple problems as machinery bogged down in mud, roads flooded and rail tracks washed out, all of which created unsafe conditions for the workers.[103] When work became impossible, newly hired men became newly unemployed men, as much of the construction could not be done in such bad weather.[104] With no jobs, these men had no money, and their basic needs of food and shelter often went unmet. A reporter for the county newspaper stated, "There was a lot of hungry men in Mineral Wells during this past week. They had no money and no place to sleep. They had come on a shoestring to work, and it was soon used up."[105] The weather also caused the December draft call to be moved to January so that there was time to finish the facilities before the men started arriving.[106]

Despite the soggy start, good things were still happening. The War Department jointly awarded the firms of General Engineering Corporation and Wallace Plumbing a $1 million contract to provide all the heating, cold

Rain, mud and frustrated workers battled the weather. *U.S. Army Speedometer*, 1941. *Courtesy Palo Pinto County Newspapers Collection, Boyce Library, Special Collections.*

storage and steam distribution for the camp; this was expected to bring one thousand more new jobs.[107] Shotts Electric Company of Fort Worth and Fishback and Moore of New York were contracted to install a $700,000 electrical system to the camp.[108] Striplings Dairy barn, across from the camp, was sold and converted into a boardinghouse for workers; another planned development included a trailer camp adjoining the property.[109] The Imperial Auction Company sold 638 home sites by auction the week of January 20, 1941.[110] Tommy Y. Fee, "the only Chinese American in Mineral Wells," announced that he bought the Oxford Café and would specialize in "chop suey and good American food."[111] Local mattress maker, Karl Walker, had so much business that he was working from 6:00 a.m. to 11:00 p.m. for weeks on end. He averaged making seventy-five to one hundred mattresses per week.[112]

When the mud receded to "ankle depth,"[113] most of the men were able to start back to work, except the construction quartermaster, who was replaced by Major Paul M. Brewer (January 2, 1941).[114] When Major Brewer took over, the camp was 10 percent complete.[115] He brought in a multitude of workers to complete the project. Included in the new workers were a mass of eighteen thousand laborers (union and nonunion) and hundreds of auxiliary personnel (e.g., forty stenographers had been brought in from Fort Sam Houston), and they "dug-in."[116]

All main contractors had offices located at the camp, and many of the executives from these companies were there daily.[117] Mr. F.M. "Cap" Reeves of F.M. Reeves and Sons was there "almost twenty-four hours of every day," and their building superintendent (O.K. Johnson) was there "eighteen hours a day to insure its rapid and successful completion."[118] Workers labored around the clock. There were three shifts (Dawn Patrol, Day Crew and Night Crew); large floodlights were brought in to assist workers; materials started arriving again (thirty-five to fifty train carloads

Left: Construction Quartermaster Brewer. *U.S. Army Speedometer*, 1941. *Courtesy Palo Pinto County Newspapers Collection, Boyce Ditto Library, Special Collections.*

Below: F.M. Reeves, general contractor of Camp Wolters, and son Hunt Reeves, 1941. *Courtesy, Fort Worth Star-Telegram Collection, October 1940, Special Collections, University of Texas at Arlington Libraries.*

Opposite: Construction workers framing buildings at Camp Wolters. *Courtesy Fort Worth Star-Telegram Collection, December 1940, Special Collection, University of Texas at Arlington Libraries.*

per day); and huge machines cut down trees, moved tons of rock and dirt and started transforming a hilly wooded area into an army camp.[119]

Major Brewer's first group of military personnel arrived on February 15, and they shifted construction into high gear.[120] The major installed a work "thermometer" sign at the front of the camp that indicated the level of completeness, the very top of the thermometer being dated March 15. By January 5, the camp was 24 percent complete; by February 1, it was

45 percent; and by March 1, it was 85 percent complete.[121] The workers kept working, the train cars kept bringing in material and the breakneck speed kept up until March 11, when the first soldiers started arriving.[122] All totaled, more than 25,920,000 cubic feet of dirt was moved; thirty-five miles of gravel, asphalt and pavement were laid; and 644 buildings were built.[123] Under Major Brewer, it was said that the Camp Wolters workforce set an all-time construction record for speed with the construction of the new camp.[124]

The total cost for the project was between $12 million and $14.2 million.[125] There were no work-related fatalities, and there were few work-related accidents.[126] The Cage and Reeves payroll clerks processed "16,000 pay-roll checks in one day and issued 14,000 in one hour and twelve minutes."[127] Workmen were paid after work every Saturday.[128] The first time that the weekly payroll for Cage and Reeves hit $400,000, it made headlines across the state.[129] Headlines were made again on January 24, 1941, when the weekly payroll hit $646,000.[130] Headlines were made for a third time when the payroll exceeded $850,000 for the week of January 31. Major Brewer said it was the largest weekly payroll in Texas.[131] This brought nationwide attention to Camp Wolters and Mineral Wells.

Colonel Fay W. Brabson assumed charge of Camp Wolters on January 1, 1941, and began preparing for the arrival of the first group of trainees,

Cage and Reeves office staff. *U.S. Army Speedometer*, 1941. *Courtesy Palo Pinto County Newspapers Collection, Boyce Ditto Library, Special Collections.*

due March 15. An additional 1,000 soldiers joined him in February from Fort Sam Houston to act as trainers for the men.[132] Lieutenant Colonel Charles Hall joined Colonel Brabson's staff on February 2 as quartermaster, and Lieutenant Colonel Arthur Lang was made quartermaster executive officer.[133] On February 3, thirty-six noncommissioned officers arrived from Fort Sill. More arrived on February 15 and February 17, bringing the total to 3,500 men preparing for the first group of trainees.[134]

The large installation encountered several problems, some dramatic and others more tedious in character. A fifty-one-year-old German alien was arrested trying to get into the camp with "a quantity of highly flammable chemicals on his person and incendiary sticks."[135] The FBI investigated the German, B.W. Ehrlich, for sabotage.[136] He had tried to get work at the camp under several false names but had been rejected; he also carried multiple social security cards. He was in custody at the Palo Pinto County jail pending charges. Ehrlich's arrest cranked up the fear and anxiety about possible enemy sympathizers in the area. The local people had already been on the watch for people with pro-German sentiment since the previous May (1940). At that time, a "foreigner" had pulled into a Mineral Wells gas station asking for directions to the small community of Poseidon. In the back seat of the car were "hundreds of pamphlets that were pro-German and had the names of other small communities on them that were known to have a German population."[137] The arrest of the German resulted in a mass community meeting being called for on June 21, 1941, at the Mineral Wells American Legion Hall. There they discussed local defenses, possible "Fifth Columnists" and how people were to be dealt with that exhibited anti-U.S. behavior and formed a defense council that would "chase down" any possible threat to the community or country.[138] This new threat greatly upset the citizens of Mineral Wells, and they renewed their determination to root out any person that could threaten the camp or the nation at large. The FBI and local authorities were unable to find any additional evidence of sabotage on Ehrlich and released the German.[139] A steel fence was placed around the camp later in the year.[140]

On February 4, a woman was kidnapped from Camp Wolters, forced to leave with her armed assailant and go to Weatherford (a nearby town). Leona Lansford was sitting in her car at the camp waiting to take a friend into Mineral Wells when a man with a pistol approached, forced his way into the car and took off. She was able to escape from her captor when they had to stop for gas. Miss Lansford ran screaming to the gas attendant, and her assailant fled. The assailant was thought to be bank robber and jail escapee Robert Hill.[141]

If possible Fifth Columnists and a kidnapping were not enough to keep Colonel Brabson's attention, he also encountered the problem of fire. On February 22, a paint sprayer exploded and started a fire that damaged the $125,000 cold storage building. The building was 95 percent completed.[142] Thankfully, only minimal damage was done.

Traffic was a massive problem in the city and on Highway 80 by the camp. Captain E.M. Wells of the Texas State Highway Patrol said, "This stretch of highway has become the most dangerous area in Texas. Traffic has multiplied to such an extent that is almost unmanageable."[143] This was the main roadway between Weatherford and Mineral Wells. The roads were long and straight in this area, and it was tempting for people to drive at excessive speeds. Captain Wells said that the normal drive between Mineral Wells and Fort Worth was an hour, but due to the increase in traffic, it had become four hours, which people were not taking into consideration when they started out.[144] Multiple proposals and options were discussed on what could be done about the traffic problem.[145] People could become stuck in their cars for over an hour during high traffic times. Some parked their cars on the shoulder of the road, walked and came back for their cars later. People often became frustrated and upset. On one occasion, a camp worker driving from his home in Fort Worth to the camp became stuck in such a jam and decided to pass cars on the right (emergency) side, which was illegal. While doing this, he made a face and stuck out his tongue at the woman in the car in front of him. This infuriated the woman, and after getting out of the traffic jam, she reported the worker to the county constable and demanded his arrest. The constable found the driver and ticketed him with passing on the right-hand side. The man protested the charge, but he later owned up to it and paid the fine.[146] The State Highway Patrol commented that they had given out 107 tickets, quadruple the number of tickets as normal, between January 1 and February 5, 1941. Additionally, nine people died, thirty-seven wrecks occurred and seventy arrests required bookings.[147] The State Highway Patrol added two more patrolmen to the area, bringing a total of six patrolmen to this strip of Highway 80.[148] On May 12, a soldier was killed on this highway trying to board a bus.[149]

Saturday night was the biggest night of the week during this time in Mineral Wells. Most camp workers were paid Saturday evening, and with the "weekly payroll of more than $900,000 the last three months have brought super-prosperity to the city."[150] The banks, barbershops, restaurants and merchants stayed open late to assist the newly moneyed workers. Before the doors closed, merchants had empty shelves; restaurants were sold out; tired waiters and waitresses were rubbing their feet, their pockets bulging with tip money; and the local jail had filled with drunks.[151]

The county paper often carried stories about the problems alcohol caused. On the weekend of January 11–12, 1941, thirty-seven men were arrested for drunkenness.[152] Palo Pinto County sheriff Edmonson had to refuse a "carload" full of women charged with vagrancy from the Mineral Wells Police Department on February 22. The sheriff stated that his jail was full and had no more room for "boarders" at the time. In the county jail at that moment were ten Camp Wolters workers who were arrested for gambling, a soldier trying to sell a government overcoat, the man who was going to buy it and over a dozen drunks.[153]

In response to a story that the *Fort Worth Press* printed, that "the biggest mythical influenza outbreak in American history" happened at Camp Wolters with people selling a "flu" medication at the camp, the *Palo Pinto County Star* decided to set the record straight and explain what this "flu" medication was. The medication was "whiskey." Camp Wolters was in a dry county, with legal sales available only to those who were sick and asked for a whiskey prescription at the drugstore. During the month of January 1941, the combined total of whiskey prescriptions sold in Mineral Wells was 15,833.[154]

A wave of counterfeit checks bearing the name of construction companies working at the camp were cashed by multiple stores in Mineral Wells, Weatherford and Fort Worth during the week of February 24. The total amount drawn on the Cage Bros. and F.M. Reeves and Sons account totaled $843.38. All checks were written for the same three amounts: $62.11, $79.20 and $89.10. The sheriff and Major Dot Smith of Camp Wolters

DAN'S VENETIAN CLUB
MINERAL WELLS, TEXAS

"Dan's Venetian Club," a Mineral Wells restaurant during World War II that was popular with officers from Wolters. *From https://www.ebay.com/itm/10xDANS-VENETIAN-CLUB-Mineral-Wells-Texas-Roadside-1940s-Vintage-Linen-Postcard-/273797993856.*

warned local merchants and bankers about the situation.[155] Two of the merchants that cashed the forged checks were the Army Store and Dan's Venetian Club.[156] The forgers were eventually caught. Mr. and Mrs. E.M. Landrum were arrested in Victoria, Texas, and returned to the county jail. Mrs. Landrum was released on bail, but Mr. Landrum was not. Mr. E.M. Landrum received two years in the penitentiary for this crime.[157]

The food servers in Mineral Wells went on strike during the weekend of February 15 and 16. Led by the Hotel and Restaurant Employees International Alliance No. 760 and Bar Tenders International League of America, the workers went on strike because they could no longer afford to pay rent on their current salary. The waiters demanded a minimum wage of $0.30 an hour, and the waitresses demanded $0.25 per hour.[158] Results of the strike are unknown.

As the camp neared completion, more officials began to visit. Brigadier General Joseph Atkins, chief of staff of the Third Army Corps, visited on February 21, and W.H. Harrison of the National Defense Advisory Commission visited on March 2. Mr. Harrison stated, "This is one of the best and most complete replacement camps I have visited."[159] He congratulated the workers and staff on a job well done. As the end of construction grew closer, more men were being released from work. As of February 24, there were only 11,223 workers left at camp.[160] On March 7, Camp Wolters was visited by Mexican general Miguel Henríquez Guzmán, commander of the Seventh Military Zone for Mexico. He came to Camp Wolters to see a "sample of what America is doing in its preparedness program."[161]

While visiting Camp Wolters, General Henríquez Guzmán admired the firing range that was still being built. The firing range was one of the largest in the nation. Its construction required the removal of 500,000 yards of dirt and the pouring of 30,000 yards of concrete. The range was 3,100 feet long and 1,800 feet wide. The range had 250 targets and was equipped for rifle, machine gun, trench mortar and antiaircraft fire. There was also space reserved for grenade practice. Men worked in ten-hour shifts to get the range ready. The range was ready by March 15. The cost was estimated to be $300,000.[162]

With the deadline for the camp coming quickly into view, Mother Nature decided to step in once again and slow things down. On March 1, it started raining, bringing ice-cold winds and snow flurries. The rain continued for six days, bringing outside work to a standstill. Interior workers continued around-the-clock hours and made great progress with the bakery and radio station nearing completion. They had just broken ground on the laundry facility when the rain began to fall. Despite the setback, the camp still expected the first arrival of selectees sometime between March 11 and March 20. Minor construction continued when the first selectees arrived.[163]

When the camp was near completion, Washington requested that the construction quartermaster Major Paul Brewer take another position. Major Brewer took over as construction quartermaster on January 1 and set an army construction record for speed with Camp Wolters. Only 10 percent of the work was completed when he started, and by March 6, it was 87.5

The firing range. In *A Camera Trip through Camp Wolters: A Picture Book of the Camp and Its Activities. Courtesy A.F. Weaver Collection, Boyce Ditto Library, Special Collections.*

Service Club postcard. *Courtesy Willie H. Casper Jr.*, Pictorial History of Fort Wolters, *vol. 1,* Infantry Replacement Training Center, *1940, Boyce Ditto Library, Special Collections.*

percent complete. Appointed acting construction quartermaster, Captain Houston Gaddy oversaw the camp to completion.[164] Before his departure, a testimonial dinner was given for Major Brewer at the Baker Hotel by the CoC.[165] At the dinner, it was stated that Major Brewer had "pulled the camp out of the mire…to win one of the greatest battles against time and the elements ever recorded in the annals of Texas Construction history."[166]

Captain Jay Russell, chief architect for Camp Wolters, made use of the newly finished Service Club on March 8 and presented gold watches to the four men responsible for getting the camp built: Captain F.M. Reeves (general contractor), Will O'Connell (general manager), O.K. Johnson (general superintendent) and Sam Owens (first assistant general superintendent).[167]

The building of the camp had tested the determination of the workmen, contractors, store owners, citizens of the county, banks and local government. Mother Nature did not cooperate with the construction. She threw almost everything she had at them and was most assuredly their biggest obstacle. However, the men and women involved in this project kept coming back day after day, unwilling to be defeated. Their tenacity won as the camp opened in time. This Herculean effort would not be in vain; seventeen thousand men would soon be arriving to put the new facilities to use. With construction finished, the work of war began.

Chapter 3

THE INFANTRY REPLACEMENT TRAINING SYSTEM

The monumental effort put forth by the construction workers of Camp Wolters was microscopic in comparison to the job that the army was just starting. The army, numbering 189,839 men in 1939,[168] was about to start growing at an exponential rate that did not stop until the end of the war in 1945, when the army numbered 8,267,958.[169] This expansion was spearheaded by General George C. Marshall, army chief of staff. He led an experienced group of army men, all of whom had seen battle during World War I, and knew intimately the problems of war and, specifically, the problems with the replacement system. They created a new replacement system to end the problems of the past and act as a springboard to catapult the replacements into the position they needed to be in when their time came to take over. The army experienced many issues implementing this system and hired experts at the end of the war to evaluate the program and make recommendations for improvements.

When the army's experiment with Replacement Training Centers (RTCs) began, neither the army nor the soldiers knew exactly what to expect. The army had planned and made projections, but until the first replacement training soldier was put into the field, nobody knew if this system worked. Everyone had a positive outlook when training started, the soldiers worked long, hard hours to be ready when called, and the army provided them with everything that it thought a soldier needed. However, the RTC system encountered many unforeseen problems that continued to be a burden throughout the war. It is important to understand the replacement system concept and its importance to the army. Rather than an in-depth look at the overall replacement system, this chapter reflects briefly on the replacement training process and concentrates on how the army implemented it at Wolters. This overview helps explain why Wolters was established and what was expected from the men at Wolters.

Marshall and his staff agreed that the RTCs needed to be established here, on the homefront, so that when the replacements arrived overseas, they would be ready for action. There were various kinds of RTCs; some were for the cavalry, signal corps, infantry, field artillery and many other groups.[170] Camp Wolters was the largest of four IRTCs that opened in 1941.[171] General Lesley McNair, chief of staff and later commander (1942) for Army Ground Forces (AGF), designed the training programs that were used in the Replacement Training Centers.[172] The replacement soldiers received the same basic training as all soldiers, but their education included some type of specialty training. The number of replacements that were needed was based on the Table of Organization.[173] This table showed how many soldiers were required for mobilization and estimated how many losses could be expected in battle.[174] These numbers would fluctuate throughout the war and were not very reliable.

Just as RTCs across the nation were taking shape, General Marshall's army began to take shape. He was quick to see that the army organization for 189,839 men was not going to work for an army that would number in the millions. On March 9, 1942, General Marshall announced a reorganization of the army. The reorganization would simplify the army into four parts: (1) General Staff, (2) Army Air Forces, (3) Army Ground Forces, and (4) Army Service Forces.[175] This was agreeable to General McNair, who as commander of the AGF had control over all training.[176]

Camp Wolters was officially activated as an army installation on March 19, 1941, and was turned over to the army on March 22. Construction Quartermaster Major Paul Brewer handed over more than six thousand keys, weighing over two hundred pounds, to Colonel Brabson.[177] The opening of the camp and arrival of men was a cause for celebration and concern for the army. The army was more than ready to begin training its badly needed troops, but there was concern in that it had never used the RTC system before. The system was tried on a limited basis during the simulated conditions of the Louisiana maneuvers of September 1941. While reviewers offered recommendations to address issues found in the replacement system, they were apparently insufficient under combat conditions, as communications issues once again arose. Most issues with the replacement system can be boiled down to problems of communication. The army also had concerns about the vast numbers of soldiers to be trained, specifically if they had enough men to train them, as the situations in Europe and the Pacific were rapidly heating up; they had no time to waste.[178]

Training at Wolters officially began on March 24, 1941.[179] With the training cycle being thirteen weeks, the camp could achieve an output of 64,000 trainees yearly if at full capacity during all training cycles.[180] This meant that Wolters was designed to produce in one year a third of the original army size. The first group of selectees at Wolters was limited to half capacity, 9,000 men, as there were only 225 regular officers and 1,446 enlisted men available at camp to train the men. When fully staffed with 2,407 officers and enlisted men, the camp could train at full capacity, or 17,000 men.[181] Most of the reserve officers went through a special training course at Fort Benning, Georgia, in preparation for their new assignment. Wolters had seventeen battalions, training battalions Fifty-One through Sixty-Seven. The army was segregated at this time, and two of the battalions were composed of African American soldiers, battalions Sixty-Six and Sixty-Seven.[182]

Selectees began arriving at Wolters as early as March 11, 1941, when the first arrivals of 181 African American selectees entered the Camp Wolters depot.[183] The two companies from Oklahoma arrived in six sleeper cars and detrained in time for breakfast. Colonel Brabson greeted the group, mustered them into the Sixty-Sixth Training Battalion and marched them toward the mess hall.[184] More arrived daily until there were nine full battalions.

When the selectee arrived, he underwent a thirteen-week basic training course, received his battalion assignment and was given a camp handbook.[185] The thirteen-week course consisted of "seven fundamental military requirements" and specialized training.[186] These were the building blocks that all training proceeded from. The first requirement was learning the basic rules of military life and elementary military training, which included instruction in discipline, courtesy, hygiene, close order drill, interior guard duty and familiarization with the Articles of War and Army Regulations. The second requirement was caring for and maintaining weapons in the field. The third requirement was to be in adequate physical condition. The fourth requirement concerned the use of weapons. The fifth requirement was a course on chemical weapons. The sixth requirement involved the use of various kinds of maps and techniques in concealment. The last requirement was to practice the duties of a soldier in various locations. This requirement often involved overnight trips to different training areas that

Lessons included how to maintain and care for your equipment in the field. *Courtesy* Fort Worth Star-Telegram *Collection, August 9, 1941, Special Collections, University of Texas at Arlington Libraries.*

were designed to look like the different theaters of operation, the terrain of France, European cities and jungles of Asia. The soldiers also learned a specialized skill, such as radio operation, clerical duties, cooking, auto mechanics and defense against aircraft and mechanized units (tanks).[187]

As the men trained, the camp continued to grow. In March, the army announced that it was planning to expand Wolters to twice its present size with construction beginning in June.[188] In April, it signed a lease for eight thousand more acres and, the next day, announced that a one-thousand-man Reception Center would be included in the expansion.[189] The cost of the new construction was estimated at $496,300.[190] That was not the end of growth at Wolters. Over the course of six years, the camp built sports arenas, chapels, motor repair shops, dayrooms, storage buildings, mess halls, more barracks, service clubs and much more. The camp came to dwarf neighboring Mineral Wells. Construction was an ever-present reality in the life of the camp until the end of the war.

The first training group ended, and soldiers began shipping out on June 17 to their duty stations. General Marshall worried about this step of the process. He was concerned that when the selectees finished their training they would be used to flesh out the staff at noncombat installations instead of being sent to actual combat units.[191] General Marshall was correct; this did happen and was one of multiple problems in the replacement system. The camp prepared for its first full-capacity training cycle to begin on July 1, when seventeen thousand men were to be in camp.[192]

Originally, the men that were selected for the draft had a duty obligation of twelve months' service. As the situation in both Europe and the Pacific continued to crumble, this caused the president and military leaders much concern, as the first selectees were completing their service just as war seemed imminent.[193] On August 18, FDR signed the Selective Service Extension Act.[194] This act increased the selectees' army service from twelve months to thirty months.[195] This act passed Congress by one vote. It was unpopular with many people, and many grumbled about it. Some soldiers threatened to desert after their twelve months were up. When asked about the attitudes of selectees coming into service since the length of service had changed, General Simpson, commander of Camp Wolters, said that the morale of men entering the army was high. He stated, "They are men. Men of purpose and vision and patriotism. And none of them likes to hear the plea of the tearful appeaser as he pities their plight and demands that they be sent back home to mamma."[196] General Simpson insisted that it was civilian morale that needed attention, not his troops'.

General Simpson was not the only person concerned with morale. In an address at Trinity College in 1941, General Marshall himself said, "It is the morale that wins the victory. Morale is a state of mind. It is a steadfastness and courage and hope. With it all things are possible, without it everything else, planning, preparation, production, count as naught."[197] With that in mind, Marshall tried to ensure the morale of his army was high at all times.[198] Each camp had a morale officer and a recreation officer. Captain Roy T. Falkenburg was the first morale officer at Wolters, and Lieutenant J.O. McMahan was the first recreation officer.[199] Together, they worked hard to keep up the men's spirits and have them enjoy their off-duty time. They offered the men the ability to enjoy a variety of activities.

General William Hood Simpson, first commander of Camp Wolters, 1941. *Courtesy Fort Worth Star-Telegram Collection, 1941, Special Collections, University of Texas at Arlington Libraries.*

If it was baseball, you also could play with a league team, or, on Sundays, watch the Camp Wolters Doughboys in action.

The Camp Wolters Doughboys. *Courtesy Willie H. Casper Jr.*, Pictorial History of Fort Wolters, *vol. 1*, Infantry Replacement Training Center, *1940, Boyce Ditto Library, Special Collections.*

The most popular activities were dancing, watching movies and athletics, with baseball, basketball, football and boxing garnering the most participants. There were weekly dances and three movie theaters, and during the season, there were intercamp games and boxing competitions. These often drew large crowds and were extremely popular. The first intercamp baseball game was played at Wolters on April 11, 1942. The Doughboy Nine went against the 120th Quartermaster Regiment representing Camp Berkley. Heading the lineup for Wolters was Private Charley Stanceu of the 62nd Battalion, who had pitched for the World Champion New York Yankees the year before, and Private Dick Midkiff, former pitcher for Baltimore.[200]

The army also enlisted the help of Hollywood in raising the morale of soldiers and civilians by producing such movies as *Sergeant York* (1941), *They Died with Their Boots On* (1942) and *Casablanca* (1942). These are just a few of the multitude of war films Hollywood cranked out during the war years that were seen in the camp theaters. Hollywood went a step further and sent movie stars to army camps to entertain the soldiers. Wolters had its first group of visiting celebrities the weekend of June 21 and 22, 1941. Chico Marx arrived with a "Pullman-load of talent," including Harry Savoy, Toni Lane, Janice Williams, Marjorie Gainesworth and Tommy Trant.[201] That was just the beginning; other celebrities who visited were Judy Garland and husband David Rose,[202] Carmen Miranda, Dale Evans, Joan Blondell and Bill Holden, among many others, including professional boxers Joe Louis and Sugar Ray Robinson, who put on an exhibition match. Samuel Goldwyn, Hollywood producer and director, visited the camp and spoke with men when his son was stationed at Wolters. He emphasized the importance of movies in keeping up the morale of the soldiers.[203]

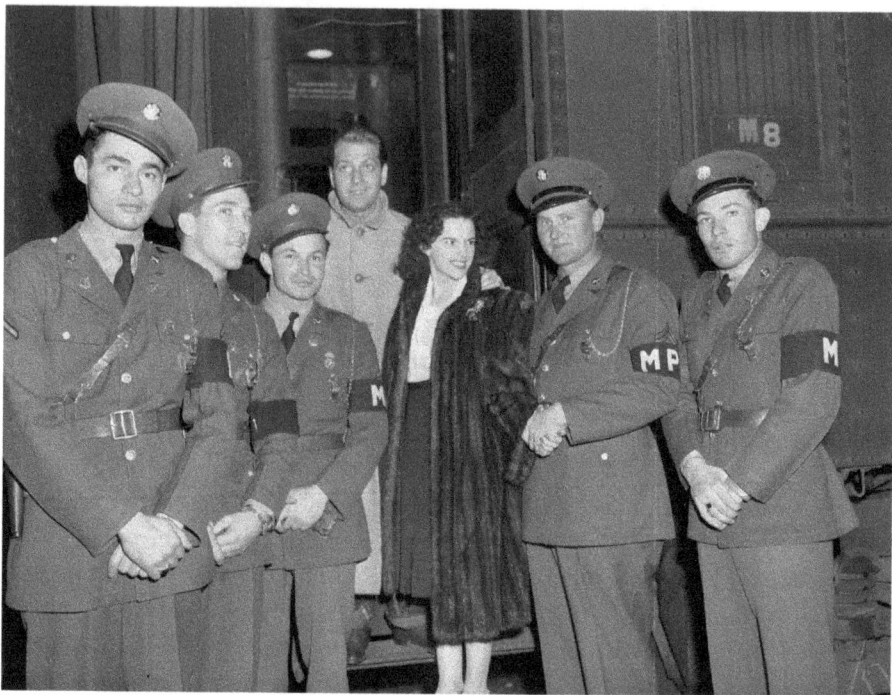

Judy Garland arrives at Wolters with husband David Rose. *Courtesy* Fort Worth Star-Telegram *Collection, January 30, 1942, Special Collections, University of Texas at Arlington Libraries.*

The seriousness of the situation struck home on December 7, 1941, as Japanese planes bombed the U.S. Pacific Fleet at Pearl Harbor and war was quickly declared. Richard Scholl, a selectee at Wolters at the time, was on a weekend pass and stayed overnight in Fort Worth with a friend. That Sunday, they were at a movie theater when it was announced that Pearl Harbor had been attacked and all military personnel were to return to their base immediately. When the theater audience received the news, he said everyone was shocked. That was his first and last leave for four years.[204] Seven officers from Wolters had already departed for duty in the Philippines on November 1, and more quickly joined them.[205]

The IRTCs kept cranking out soldiers, and all seemed to go well that first year of war. The army's main concern at this time was getting the troops trained and transported to their theater of operation.[206] However, in late 1942 and early 1943, the first indication that there was a problem with the replacement system appeared. Officers in the field sent the War Department requests for massive numbers of replacements. This concerned mostly the troops in North Africa. Units bound for the European or Mediterranean

42

theaters often stopped in North Africa to refuel and restock their supplies. North Africa was also an active theater and had its own replacement needs. Upon arrival in North Africa, many replacement soldiers bound for other locations were taken by U.S. provisional units and issued new orders that allowed the replacement soldiers to become members of the provisional unit. This redirection by the provisional units was allowed by the U.S. commanding officers only when the mission of the provisional unit was deemed critical to the overall success of the army and the unit was needed for a short period of time. After the unit completed the mission, the replacement soldiers were to go on to their original assignments.[207] However, this did not always happen, as the commanding officers in North Africa oftentimes kept the soldiers and incorporated them into regular units. This caused great confusion on the part of the War Department, and the generals who had asked for replacements never received them because communications were slow and problematic.

Another problem with the replacement system was how the army counted soldiers. An example is given by Leonard Lerwill of how soldiers on their way to India or China might stop in North Africa before continuing to their assigned base, and their total was added to the base strength amount for North Africa.[208] Strength of numbers and accounting problems continued to plague the army throughout the war.

During the summer of 1943, the army was organizing the upcoming calls for service when they realized that they were going to be short 446,000 men by the end of the year.[209] This led to a memorandum being sent to the local draft boards that they needed to reclassify the men on their rolls. The largest group that was being deferred were men aged eighteen to thirty-seven who were fathers but did not participate in agricultural work.[210] The initial decision to quit deferring this group—that is, to draft men who were fathers as long as they were not agricultural workers—caused an uproar among draft boards and the general population. One senator called for the permanent deferral of all fathers and wanted an emergency session of Congress to address only this issue.[211] The House and Senate worked out a compromise that was passed in December that fathers were to be called to service only if all other similarly classified people had already been called. Specifically, the bill states, "On a national basis, fathers maintaining a bona fide family relationship, if classified I-A, would not be called into service until all other persons in class I-A at that time had been called."[212] The resulting draft enlisted only 90,000 more men, which fell far short of the number needed. The Selective Service failed to provide an adequate number of men for the armed services during the period of September 1, 1943–April 30, 1944, according to Lerwill, and the number was not small. The Selective Service failed to send 443,967 men.[213]

In July 1943, the army announced that basic training was being extended a week and officer training school extended by one month.[214] The camp newspaper, the *Camp Wolters Longhorn*, claimed that this change was being done to "round out" the soldiers' training. There had been earlier complaints about the quality of the soldiers coming out of the IRTCs and that they needed more training. A meeting was called in Washington, D.C., to discuss the replacement problem in May. At the conclusion of that meeting, it was decided that "training currently conducted in Replacement Training Centers was not adequate."[215] There was much discussion about how long to extend the training and what additional training to include. The decision was made to add an extra week to training, but that was later revised in August to a seventeen-week cycle.[216] The additional weeks were to be spent on field training and tactics.[217]

Some of the improvements made at Wolters due to this change was the inclusion of training at a "German Village" that had been set up at Hell's Bottom, one of the camp's training grounds. This training focused on hand-to-hand combat and mentally preparing the soldiers for street fighting.[218] The trainees also spent two straight weeks "in the field" going from one training exercise to another to help build up stamina and strength.[219] Four eleven-ton tanks were delivered to Wolters by the end of July to assist with training.[220] Next they added a new machine gun range, a bayonet trainer and a flame thrower for the soldiers to use.[221]

In the early months of 1944, the shortage of replacement soldiers became critical. The army severely curtailed the Army Specialized Training Programs (ASTP) in February 1944 to have more men in the field.[222] By April, they hoped to graduate 10,000 ASTP men per month, which would add to the army's dwindling numbers.[223] They also discontinued recruitment in the RTCs for any special program, such as paratroopers or Coast Guard. All army theaters were to fill vacancies with able-bodied men, who were to be retrained in the field and leave their jobs (clerks, communications, supply) to the men of limited assignment.[224] The reassignment and graduation of men from the ASTP program proceeded at a rapid pace. On February 25, the camp newspaper reported that by April 1, 110,000 men from the program would be reassigned for active duty.[225]

In April 1944, representatives from the North African and European theaters reported to Washington to discuss the replacement crisis. This

Hell's Bottom
Training Area,
January 2, 1944.
*Courtesy Willie
H. Casper Jr.,*
Pictorial History
of Fort Wolters,
vol. 1, Infantry
Replacement
Training Center,
*1940, Boyce Ditto
Library, Special
Collections.*

resulted in the directive of May 4, 1944, that went to all theaters, including the Pacific. In the directive, the army gave very specific and clear instructions on how to count classifications of men, ordered them to create and maintain a replacement pool, added medical personnel to help determine a soldier's fitness for duty and created personnel audit teams.[226] The Army Air Forces also returned thirty thousand men who had not completed pilot training to the army.[227] These measures patched the replacement situation briefly, but a permanent solution was still needed.

In December 1944, the War Department called another meeting about the replacement crisis. The United States was in the heaviest fighting of the war, and casualties were taking a substantial toll; replacements were badly needed. After days of discussion, it was decided that the European theater would call in 10,000 of its men from the air force and 20,000 of its men from the communications zone, retrain them and place them in the field.[228] In January 1945, it was reported that 80,000 men from the Army Air Forces and Army Service Forces had been transferred to AGF for field training.[229] In February, there was a shortage of training instructors at Wolters;[230] this caused some army officials to worry about the quality of training and resulted in a personal inspection of the camp by the new AGF commander, General Joseph Stillwell.[231] An example of the replacement crisis can be found in the Twelfth Army Group, led by General Omar Bradley.[232] They reported on May 9, 1945, as having had 745,114 casualties but had received only 700,285 replacements.[233] The reassignment and retraining of soldiers did not solve the problem, but time would.

While the audits, redirected forces and inspections helped, it was ultimately developments in the war that mitigated the situation. On May 8, 1945, at 5:01 p.m. Camp Wolters time, the war in Europe was declared over. Thousands of men at camp gathered on Scott Hill and listened as their leaders spoke of the war in Europe. They also reminded the men that the war with Japan was not over, that further sacrifices were to be made and that not everyone was going home. The camp band played the National Anthem, and Chaplain Robert Hardee said a prayer.[234]

With the war in Europe over, the army now put all its manpower into fighting the war with Japan. The replacement problem was still an issue but not near what it had been and was put on the back burner for the moment. General Marshall hired Dr. E.P. Learned and Dr. Dan T. Smith on June 9, 1945, to study the replacement problem and make suggestions.[235] The study's conclusions were wide-ranging. They noted that the army had not appropriately planned personnel or resources, there were too many agencies involved in the process of getting replacements, that replacements were often diverted from original assignments and that the various theaters and commanders were not as involved in the process as they should be.[236] The study presented multiple suggestions that could be started right away to address these problems.

The suggestions made by the Learned-Smith study did not have an opportunity to take effect, as victory over Japan came rapidly. News of the defeat came the evening of Tuesday, August 14. The camp had a ceremony the next day, and several smaller ceremonies were conducted at the camp chapels.[237]

With the war over, people worried about the future of Wolters. The soldiers were not sure if they could go home or be sent overseas as part of the occupation. They wondered if the camp would continue to train soldiers. Many of the civilian workers worried about the loss of their jobs. This was a time of uncertainty and anxiety for many. Initially, the trainees kept training and the civilians kept working. Yet within a month, camp administrators began making small cuts in the civilian workforce,[238] with most employees remaining on in some capacity until the end of the year.[239]

As Camp Wolters started winding down operations, the camp's long-term fate was still uncertain. Soldiers went home or were transferred, battalions were combined for lack of soldiers, a Separation Point was opened and closed and the IRTC accepted its last, and smallest, class in November and

Photograph of the ceremony at Scott Hill on V-E Day. *Courtesy* Camp Wolters Longhorn, *May 11, 1945, 3, microfilm from Boyce Ditto Library, Special Collections.*

then closed in December.[240] The camp newspaper issued its last edition on December 28, 1945.[241]

January 1946 was a devastating month for the camp. On January 6, the service clubs closed, and on January 19, the IRTC was inactivated; by January 23, the army had announced that Wolters was surplus.[242] This was quite a blow to the people of Mineral Wells. On January 31, army engineers arrived, took over and started dismantling the camp.[243]

It took the next several months to pull down, transfer, clean up and sell the various parts of the camp that remained. The POW camp was one of the last groups to leave. The POWs were transferred to Camp Bowie in Brownwood, Texas, on April 5. On August 15, the flag came down for the last time at Camp Wolters.

The replacement system trained 2,500,000 soldiers, or 30 percent of the 1945 army total.[244] Camp Wolters trained between 200,000 and 250,000 soldiers, or 8 to 10 percent of the total replacement system force.[245] The exact

Closing ceremony at Camp Wolters. *Courtesy* Fort Worth Star-Telegram *Collection, August 15, 1946, Special Collections, University of Texas at Arlington Libraries.*

number of men trained at Wolters is unknown. There are two sources that can be relied on for accuracy; one is the *Fort Worth Star-Telegram's* interview with Colonel Edward Coing, the last commander of Wolters, on the day Camp Wolters closed. He set the number at "more than 250,000 soldiers."[246] In the article, he commented, "More than a quarter of a million were taught here."[247] The second source, the camp newspaper, the *Camp Wolters Longhorn*, offered a slightly lower number. In its final issue, on the front page, it states that "nearly 200,000 civilians" were trained.[248]

On peak capacity, numbers range greatly, though no official tally was found. Colonel Willie Casper, who was a commander of Fort Wolters in the 1960s, states that Wolters "housed as many as 30,000 soldiers at one time."[249] However, in the same book but a different article, he set the number as "50,000."[250] David Minor, writing for the *Handbook of Texas Online*, sets the number at 24,973.[251] An estimate of 25,000 to 30,000 seems appropriate.

There are also a variety of answers about how large the camp was in acreage. Most sources state that Camp Wolters was 7,500 acres.[252] It did start out with 7,500 acres in 1941, but it started leasing more land almost as soon as it opened.[253] The Camp Wolters IRTC Handbook of 1941 states that the camp included 16,000 acres; however, according to Colonel Casper, the camp leased over 23,000 acres before closing in 1946.[254]

There were high hopes within the army that when Camp Wolters and other IRTCs opened, they would be the answer to the replacement problem. Camp Wolters itself was an exemplary camp, from estimations made by both the army and former soldiers.[255] However, it did not solve the replacement problem because of issues within the system. The need for experienced troops continued to worsen throughout the war, not because the camps failed in their jobs, but because the system failed to prepare adequately for the excessive growth the army had in such a short time. The army failed to recognize and anticipate even mundane problems, including how many soldiers were assigned to a battalion, how many were on leave and how many were in the hospital. Lerwill says, "Efficient use of military manpower can only be achieved when there is an effective replacement system."[256] He also notes that in every study of the replacement system since World War II a recommendation has been made to have officers trained in personnel administration and planning.[257]

World War II was an unprecedented event, and the army may not have been able to foresee the multiple problems that were encountered. The army used a different method for replacement soldiers for the next military conflict, the Korean War. Whatever the problems with the replacement system, Wolters produced battle-ready soldiers who fought hard for their country. Several won the Medal of Honor.[258] Men such as Audie Murphy, widely known as the most decorated soldier of World War II, arrived at Camp Wolters in June 1942.[259] Vernon Baker, who met southern racism for the first time when he arrived at Wolters in June 1941, was one of three African American soldiers trained at Wolters who received the Medal of Honor. The other two were Edward Carter (1941) and Charles L. Thomas (1942). The last two Medal of Honor winners were Jack L. Knight (1941) and Eli L. Whiteley (1942). The army admitted there were problems with the replacement system, but the replacement soldiers trained at Wolters were effective soldiers on the battle lines and in the defense of their country.

Chapter 4

WAR AND CHANGING TIMES

C amp Wolters was active during World War II, and segregation of the races was legally practiced in the United States during this time, especially in the South. African Americans and other nonwhite citizens were not given the same rights and respect as white citizens and were kept separated from them. This chapter looks at what evidence is left of the two African American battalions that were trained at Wolters and tries to reconstruct as much of their lives while at camp as possible.[260] It will also look at the Women's Auxiliary Army Corps (WAAC) unit that began arriving in June 1943 and what role it played at camp. Before the war, most married white women did not work outside the home, but with the men off to war, women got the opportunity to show what they could do when given a chance, but they had to fight for that chance. Lastly, the German prisoners of war who arrived in 1944 and were kept in a separated area of the camp will be discussed. These three groups all offer a different view of Wolters that the regular selectee did not get, the regular selectee being a white male U.S. citizen. As their challenges were different from those of enlisted or fully employed white men, they provide by way of contrast a sense of what advantages the privileges of race and gender entailed.[261]

Before any troops arrived at Wolters, the subject of African Americans being in the army and used in combat positions was controversial.[262] The thought of African Americans with a loaded gun put fear in the hearts of many southerners.[263] Most of the newly built military camps were located in the South. Out of 118 Army training facilities across the nation, 53 were in former Confederate states.[264] Northern African Americans were not familiar with the Jim Crow traditions of the South, and most had difficulty adjusting. African American leaders requested more African Americans be allowed in the military and to serve in all areas, as opposed to limiting them to the service units. This was met with opposition from leaders who represented the South and military leaders representing the different armed branches. As late as August 1942, U.S. senators from the South were still calling for the removal of African American troops from their states.[265] The Selective Service and Training Act of 1940 set the limit for any minority group joining the army at the same proportion as that they were represented in the overall population.[266] For African Americans at this time, that was around 10 percent. Many African Americans found this threshold unfair and continued to push for higher induction limits, but they were guaranteed the ability to apply for any military position they desired.

It was a cold morning when the very first troops arrived at Wolters, March 11, 1941. These troops comprised 181 "shivering Negro boys" from Fort Sill, Oklahoma.[267] They became part of the two African American training

The first troops that arrived at Wolters were African Americans from Oklahoma. *Courtesy* Fort Worth Star-Telegram, *March 1941, Special Collections, University of Texas at Arlington Libraries.*

battalions formed at Wolters, battalions Sixty-Six and Sixty-Seven. The first commander of the Sixty-Sixth Battalion was Lieutenant Colonel William H. McCutheon, and the first executive officer was Major Hal C. Granberry, both from Fort Huachuca in Arizona.[268]

There were 1,500–2,000 African American soldiers in training at Wolters when the camp was fully functional.[269] No official number of African Americans that were trained at Wolters is extant; however, the last issue of the camp newspaper states, "There were nearly 15,000 colored troops (trained here)."[270] As in the rest of the South, segregation was a part of the African American soldiers' experience at Camp Wolters. The African American selectees were housed in Area Six in the southeast part of camp.[271] Area Six also contained a theater (Theater Three), post exchange (PX), a guesthouse, a chapel and a bus stop. The buses for the African American soldiers who connected the camp to Mineral Wells ran from 5:45 p.m. to 11:30 p.m. The buses for white soldiers ran from 5:00 a.m. to 11:30 p.m.[272] First Lieutenant S.F. Guilbeau was an African American chaplain at Wolters.[273] The African American service club was south of Area Six.[274] The Sports Arena was reserved for their use only on Thursday nights.[275]

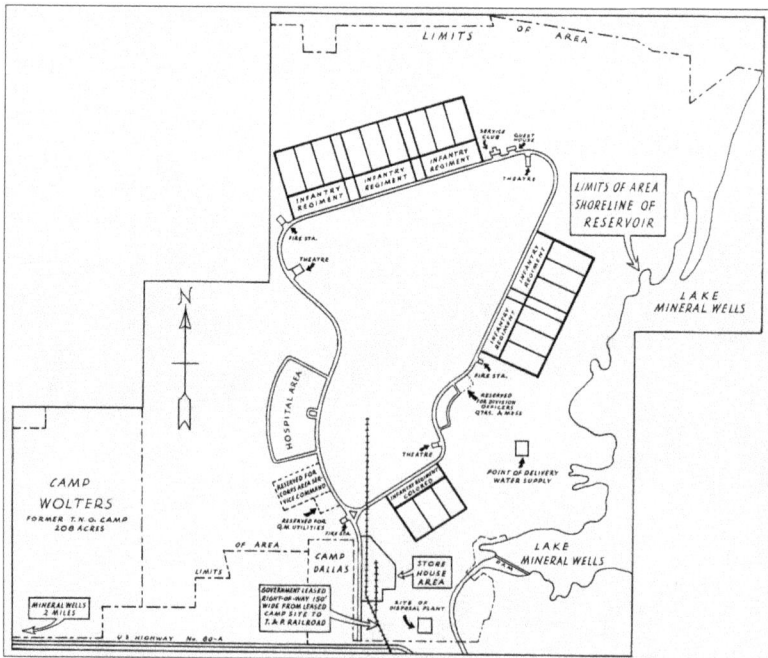

Note Area Six. *Courtesy Willie H. Casper Jr.*, Pictorial History of Fort Wolters, *vol. 1*, Infantry Replacement Training Center, *1940, Boyce Ditto Library, Special Collections.*

When the new selectees arrived at camp, the camp was in the final stages of construction. During inspection in April 1941, an officer asked if any of the new African American selectees knew how to work with wood or could do any carpentry. One man from the Sixty-Sixth Battalion came forward, Private Floyd Wise. He had some experience but was concerned that nobody else had stepped forward. The officer assigned him a crew and told him to get to work finishing the surrounding buildings. When the selectees were not drilling or involved in other training exercises, they were found working on these buildings.[276]

The first cycle of training was completed in June 1941, and the men started shipping out. The first group of 544 African American soldiers left for San Francisco to join the 394th Quartermaster Battalion. A group of 72 African American soldiers was sent to the 25th Infantry Regiment at Fort Huachuca, in Arizona.[277] A group of 535 was sent to Oakland in July.[278] Overseeing this movement and training was Colonel Louis B. Knight, who became the commander of the 66th Battalion on May 26, 1941.[279]

On June 6, 1941, the county newspaper reported the arrest of an African American soldier.[280] He was arrested for carrying "concealed weapons." It is highly possible that this soldier was military policeman (MP) Corporal George M. Shuffer Jr., who had been transferred from Fort Huachuca to Wolters to train the African American MPs. In an interview, he recounts how the first time he came into Mineral Wells, the white MPs rejected his authority, arrested him and took him back to headquarters. He was released with no apology. Corporal Shuffer later became Brigadier General Shuffer.[281]

In June 1941, an African American soldier, Private Lee C. Netherly, drowned in a stock tank while trying to save the life of a friend.[282] The soldiers (members of the Sixty-Sixth Training Battalion) were completing a night march at the Baker Hollow Maneuvering and Camping Site, northwest of Mineral Wells. The soldiers were washing and swimming when Private George C. Butler, who could not swim, fell in. Private Netherly noticed that his friend was struggling and jumped in to save his life. Private Netherly managed to get Private Butler to shore, but somehow Private Netherly fell back into the water, and his body was found ten minutes later. Private Netherly was posthumously awarded the Soldier's Medal for Heroism.[283]

Vernon J. Baker was an African American from Wyoming who arrived at Wolters in June 1941. He had grown up in an area where multiple races coexisted without much hostility or discrimination. Then he came to Camp Wolters and got his first taste of the Jim Crow South—or as he puts it, "Segregation hit me full in the face."[284] Baker gave an oral history interview

Private Lee C. Nethery drowned trying to save another soldier. *From https://www.fold3.com/ page/90211644/l-c-netherly.*

to the National World War II Museum where he discusses his initial encounter at Camp Wolters with a bus driver and how he quickly learned to "conform." When Baker entered the bus, he took a front seat. The (white) driver said, "Hey n——, get your bag and get to the back of the bus where you belong." Baker wanted to punch the driver, but an elderly African American man caught him, led him to the back of the bus and explained how life worked in the segregated South. He knew if he wanted to survive, he had to follow the rules of a segregated society, no matter how demeaning it felt. In 1945, Baker led a platoon against a heavily defended German stronghold, Castle Aghinolfi, took out a machine gun emplacement by himself and led his platoon in taking the stronghold. For his actions, he won the Bronze Star. When Baker's actions were reevaluated in 1993, an army commission found that Baker, and several other African Americans, had been racially discriminated against by the U.S. Army, and it was decided his actions should have earned him the Medal of Honor. He went to the White House in 1997 and was awarded his long-overdue award.[285]

The African American battalions did have a newspaper, the *Bugle*. The *Bugle* was founded by Sergeant Morris DuBois, editor; Corporal Clifford McFarland, associate editor; and managing editor Sergeant Hillard McFall Jr., who had been a reporter for an African American paper in Chicago, the *Chicago Defender*.[286] The reason we know about the battalion newspaper is solely because of the *Chicago Defender*. McFall, having been a former *Defender* reporter, sent back snippets of camp life that the *Defender* printed. Many of the African American soldiers were from the Chicago area, and the *Defender* often mentioned the soldiers by name who were stationed at Wolters; in return, many of the soldiers wrote back to the *Defender*. The *Defender* mentioned Wolters at least weekly, if not more often. Almost all the information we have about the African American troops at Camp Wolters comes from the *Defender*. The fact that the *Bugle* existed speaks to the vibrancy of the African American community at the camp and to the marginalization and separateness of the time.

Despite the excellent job Mineral Wells had done to entertain and provide recreational activities for the white soldiers, little had been done to provide similar opportunities for the African American selectees. One example is

Medal of Honor recipient Vernon J. Baker faced racism and segregation at Wolters. *Courtesy National WWII Museum, https://www. nationalww2museum.org/ war/articles/medal-of-honor-recipient-vernon-baker.*

Army Day in Mineral Wells, April 7, 1941. The town had a huge celebration for Camp Wolters with entertainment, food and dances lasting all day and well into the night.[287] However, this was for white soldiers. According to the article in the county paper, "The colored troops were entertained by the colored people of Mineral Wells."[288] What this entailed was not described. Sometime between April and June 1941, Mineral Wells decided that it needed to provide some activities for the African American soldiers and announced in June 1941 that it was planning to build an African American recreation center.[289] It was constructed and opened on March 15, 1942.[290] A white recreation center also opened the same day; both cost $77,500 and were run by the USO.[291]

It took Mineral Wells nine months to build the African American recreation center. During that time, the War Department stepped in and provided some recreational opportunities. The War Department, knowing the importance of keeping up morale, announced in July 1941 that it was funding "Jim-Crow" service clubs for African American troops across the nation, to be built and equipped for $254,000.[292] The War Department put a rush job on the project and had them opened by September 1941.[293] In August 1941, the War Department also authorized funds for the formation of seventeen "Jim-Crow" bands.[294] At Wolters, auditions were quickly held and organized by Private C.D. Woods. The band was led by First Lieutenant Frank W. Choate. Before the end of August, another band was formed.[295]

Wolters was a temporary home to many professional African American musicians. One was Floyd Ray, an orchestra leader, who had made eight recordings with Decca Records. He was made a part of the Special Services

Department in Company D of the Sixty-Seventh Battalion.[296] He formed a "Swing Recruit" band that made quite an impression with white and African American troops alike. Ray would be assigned to the morale office in 1942 and permanently stationed at Wolters.[297]

When the Area Six Service Club opened, professionally trained painter Private Garrett Whyte created a large mural, six by sixteen feet, on the east wall. Whyte, who was trained at the prestigious Hampton Institute of Art in North Carolina, had worked as an artist and cartoonist for several national newspapers, including the *Chicago Defender*, and was the cartoonist for the *Bugle* while at camp.[298] He named his mural *In Training*, as it showed different parts of the selectee's experience at Wolters; it took three months to create.

The African American USO opened on the afternoon of October 5, 1941, in Mineral Wells. The soldiers provided their own entertainment, and as was common in white military clubs, the African American soldiers had the opportunity to dance the night away as buses loaded with African American women ready to dance arrived from various cities.[299] At the first anniversary of the African American USO, there was a large celebration. The director, Robert Wilkerson, and his associate Frances G. Elliott made sure everyone had a great time. Cake was served by the Y-Anna club, a part of the USO. Ladies from the Dallas USO came and gave a stage performance during the celebration.[300]

The Dallas African American community, and African American communities in the area, often reached out to the soldiers at Wolters. On October 13, 1941, the Camp Wolters drill team joined the parade in Dallas celebrating Negro Day at the State Fair and marched with pep squads from both schools during halftime at the Prairie View–Wiley College football game.[301] Two African American groups from Dallas visited with the soldiers at the African American USO in Mineral Wells on June 6, 1942. The group from the Psi chapter of the Iota Phi Lambda sorority performed "There's A Man in the House," and the USO Girls of Dallas welcomed and encouraged the soldiers by giving away free trips to Dallas as door prizes.[302]

Sports was a very popular way to pass the time, but the African American troops were not allowed to play with the white teams because of segregation. However, they could play against other African American teams located at various camps and even semiprofessional teams located around the North Texas area. They had some great players, and many were from the National Negro League, including Private Lafayette N. Dumas (pitcher, Memphis Red Sox, aka "Big Boy" or "Jim"), Corporal William Robinson (pitcher, played third base for St. Louis Stars, aka "Bobby"), Corporal Jake Dunn

(Joseph P. Dunn Jr., Philadelphia Stars), Bill "Doc" Savage (Memphis Red Sox), Corporal Lonnie Summers (Chicago American Giants) and Private Eldridge Mayweather (first baseman, NY Black Yankees, selected to the East-West All Star Game in 1937 and 1940).[303]

The Texas Negro League's team, the Fort Worth Black Spiders, played a baseball team composed of members from "negro soldiers stationed at Camp Wolters"[304] on August 10, 1941, at La Grave Field in Fort Worth. The "Negro soldiers from Camp Wolters" played an exhibition game with the Dallas Wonders at Rebel Stadium in Dallas in 1942. Festivities began at 5:30 p.m. with a jitterbug contest.[305] The "Camp Wolters Negro Nine" played against the Green Monarchs at Rebel Field in Dallas on April 22, 1943. Reflecting that a tradition had developed, the reporter noted that the Camp Wolters team had an exceptionally strong lineup the previous year and was expected to be hard to beat.[306]

Families of the African American selectees had the same problem with housing as white families, but possibly on a worse scale because of segregation. On August 30, 1941, the Federal Works Commission approved money for defense housing in Mineral Wells, and fifteen of the one hundred houses would go to African American soldiers and their families.[307] The name of their housing units was Huachuca Place.

William H. Hastie, a civilian aide to the secretary of war and former dean of Howard University Law School, came to inspect the African American selectees and their facilities at Camp Wolters on July 11, 1941. He inspected the current 1,400 African American soldiers and was shown the African American Service club that was being built and the African American guesthouse, which was still under construction. Hastie praised the camp and the soldiers' efficiency.[308] Hastie had been appointed by FDR to help with race relations. He later (1943) resigned in protest of the U.S. military policy of segregation and discrimination.[309] The only African American general at that time (1942) was General Benjamin O. Davis. He inspected the facilities at Wolters for African American selectees as part of a routine inspection of training camps throughout the country.[310]

In October 1941, a reporter touring four camps in Texas said that morale was high at Camp Wolters. He listened to the famous "Singing Battalion," formed by the two African American companies at Wolters. Their theme song was "John Brown's Body," and "their rendition of 'God Bless America' is a camp institution."[311] It was noted by editor Mary Whatley in the county newspaper that Mineral Wells citizens often drove out to the camp to watch the review on Saturday mornings and listen to "the colored soldiers singing

'God Bless America.'" She stated, "As we listened, we thought if everyone in the nation would sing this song as enthusiastically as they were singing it and mean every word—that no matter how many dangers lurked around this corner—America was safe."[312]

A new commander took over the Sixty-Seventh Battalion in late October 1942. Lieutenant Colonel John W. Oliver personally asked to be given command of an African American battalion.[313] Asking to command African American soldiers was not common. In fact, most of the white officers that worked with African American soldiers had been placed there because they had proved to be inept or had poor leadership skills.[314] Second Lieutenant Albert Evans, an African American soldier who came to Wolters in September 1941, states, "I've seen white officers who hardly knew how to give a marching command to a platoon. They were inept; it was pathetic."[315] Lieutenant Colonel Oliver apparently was not this kind of man. Oliver had been a commander of an interracially mixed unit at Fort Sam Houston and greatly enjoyed that experience.[316]

While entertainment and sports reflected the possible richness of the life of the African American soldiers, limitations also existed. Elsewhere in the country, violent conflicts came as early as 1941 (Fort Benning) and continued to increase until the infamous "bloody summer" of 1943.[317] No record of violence or protest has been found concerning the African American soldiers at Camp Wolters. A "disturbance" happened in Dallas on January 3, 1943, that caused the military to put Dallas "off-limits" to any African American soldier. This "disturbance" involved the arrest of seventy African American soldiers.[318] MPs stated that a mob of "more than 500 Negro soldiers" had surrounded their car during the disturbance.[319] The military allowed African American soldiers back into Dallas the next day, and an investigation began. Most of the soldiers who had been arrested came from Hensley Field, a military camp in Dallas. Those who were arrested were taken back to their headquarters and were left to face their commanding general. Thirteen of the seventy who had been arrested were facing a potential court-martial.[320] That was just the start of 1943; by the end, there was an estimated "242 racial battles in forty-seven cities."[321] Not all of these involved the military, but enough did that the calls for the African American troops to be sent out of the South became louder and louder.

During 1943, the Army Service Forces became desperate for units that could perform and fill actual labor, construction, transportation and communication positions. These types of positions (noncombat) had previously been delegated to African American soldiers.[322] The Army Ground

Forces also needed soldiers to fill numerous transportation companies. By August 1943, 30,000 African American soldiers had been sent overseas to fill these positions. By October 1943, the War Department recommended "that no further Negro combat units, other than those then active, be provided."[323] This was due to a revision of troop allocation and the inactivation of multiple units that were deemed "unneeded or less useful." The army deemed forty-three African American combat battalions as unnecessary and made them into service units. Lee states, "The disproportionately high number of Negro battalions (being deemed unneeded) was traceable to the relatively less advanced state of training among Negro units."[324] With more African Americans being sent overseas to fill the service positions, and no African Americans going to IRTCs in the South, there was a decline in racial disturbances and violence during 1944–45.[325]

In the *Fort Worth Star-Telegram* dated October 5, 1943,[326] and the camp newspaper dated October 8, 1943, it is noted that the IRTC at Wolters would stop training African American soldiers after the current cycle was over and the African American cadre were sent to other units. It gives no explanation about why the training of African American troops was being discontinued, but this was the time the order to discontinue training African Americans in combat positions was handed down; however, this was not addressed in either article.[327] The Sixty-Sixth Battalion became another white battalion, and the Sixty-Seventh Battalion became the replacement battalion. No date could be found as to when the African American battalions were shipped out; however, there is a *Fort Worth Star-Telegram* article that says, "In 1944, when Negro troops were removed from Camp Wolters,"[328] and the camp paper mentions that the Literacy School was using the former African American rooms in an article dated April 7, 1944. It can only be assumed that the soldiers left sometime between January 1, 1944, and April 7, 1944.[329]

From what evidence is left, it seems that the African American battalions had a similar experience in training as that of the white battalions, but with such scant evidence, an accurate conclusion cannot be drawn; too many pieces of the puzzle are still missing.[330] It can be said that the African American troops at Wolters rose above numerous obstacles, made their time at Wolters productive and went on to serve their country with pride and integrity.

While not as contentious as African Americans in the army, women serving in the military was a circumstance the public did not like much better. Just as African Americans have been, women have been a part of every war that the United States has ever fought, although not officially. They volunteered through different organizations (American Red Cross) and occupations (mostly nursing). On the eve of World War II, Congresswoman Edith Nourse Rogers (Republican, Massachusetts) met with General Marshall and discussed war manpower and how women could be used in certain skilled areas, thereby freeing more men for combat.[331] She introduced the Women's Army Auxiliary Corps (WAAC) bill in May 1941. Most senators and congressmen opposed the bill, and many completely dismissed the bill outright—until Pearl Harbor. Once the scope of the war and the need for human labor was clear, the bill became serious business and was passed, with concessions from both sides, and signed by FDR on May 15, 1942. Secretary of War Henry Stimson appointed Oveta Culp Hobby as WAAC director. Hobby, a native Texan and wife of former Texas governor William Hobby, immediately got things rolling with recruitment drives and setting up training centers.[332]

Though they faced doubt from their male colleagues at first, the WAAC trainees proved to be a success, and as the war progressed, calls came for more and more WAACs from all military branches.[333] The WAACs proved their worth and were accepted as part of daily military life, something that did not happen with the African American soldiers. In March 1943, Congress began discussing making the WAACs officially part of the army. In July 1943, the bill passed, and WAACs officially became Women's Army Corps (WAC). Over 150,000 women served in the army by the end of the war.[334]

An advance group of WAACs (before the name change) arrived at Camp Wolters on June 13, 1943. There were eight women, led by Second Lieutenant Hattie I. Slott and Sergeant Lena L. McMinn, both from Camp Ruston, Louisiana. They were greeted by Major Kenneth Foster, commander of the Reception Center, where most WAACs worked. There were no African American WACs at Wolters. The majority of WAACs were used as instructors for the men that could not pass the army exams; others worked in various positions throughout the camp, such as being drivers, dispatchers, clerks, translators, communications operators and more.[335] For three months, they were housed at the Baker Hotel, until temporary quarters could be prepared for them at the Reception Center.[336] They had to wait on their permanent quarters for several months, as the contract for their building was not awarded until September 4 of that year.[337] They finally moved into their permanent quarters in January 1944.[338]

More women continued arriving throughout the summer of 1943 and started becoming part of camp life. The men were uncertain about having women at an army camp, and this unease could be felt in the first few articles and interviews that the camp newspaper ran on the unit. The first article, which ran on the front page, poked fun of them because they had missed their train and had to ride in a caboose to get to camp. It was accompanied with a photo of the WAACs being carried off the caboose by soldiers.[339] The WAACs had a column in the camp newspaper to report on happenings within their unit, "WAAC News," later called "The Soldier Is a Gal." Their first column was printed on July 9, 1943.[340] In this first column, the WAACs introduced themselves, thanked everyone for welcoming them and made sure everyone knew that they had gone through the same basic training as male soldiers had, except without guns.[341] Their column was preceded by a photograph of a young lady dancing in a leotard with one leg held high up while she wore a top hat. The newspaper was quick to add their smiling faces to its pages. First Officer Ruth Chamberlain took over command of the WAACs when she arrived in August.[342] The whole detachment journeyed to Dallas on August 17, 1943, to meet with other WAACs, learn about the insurance they were eligible for as members of the army and watch a movie at the Majestic Theater on how the British and Canadian Women's Service worked.[343] The WAACs felt so comfortable at Wolters that they even took on the officers at the Reception Hall for a softball game on August 23, 1943. The officers won.[344]

On August 30, 1943, the Camp Wolters WAACs officially became WACs.[345] Major Foster held a special swearing-in ceremony for the WACs in front of the Reception Center.[346] The main USO in Mineral Wells welcomed the WACs to the army with a celebration dance that weekend.[347]

WACs, like their male colleagues, participated in many sports and recreational activities. Their sports included ping-pong, archery, badminton, volleyball and basketball.[348] Later, it would also include bowling, horseback riding, swimming, golf, tennis and competitive basketball and baseball teams.[349] Many editions of the camp newspaper would feature WACs participating in a sport, especially during the summers of 1944 and 1945 when the WACs had a competitive swim team.[350]

In November 1943, the WACs at Wolters encountered a situation that few other WAC enlisting stations had come across; a Japanese American applied to become a WAC. This woman would be the only Japanese American in the entire WAC organization if she passed her enlistment exams. She had tried twice before to enlist and had been turned down because she was too young and too short.[351] Her husband was stationed at Camp Wolters; she was a civilian employee at the PX and was well known throughout the camp.[352] Prior to her coming to Camp Wolters, she had been in a Japanese

Camp Wolters WAC Swim Team, *Camp Wolters Longhorn*, July 28, 1944. *Courtesy microfilm from Boyce Ditto Library, Special Collections.*

relocation camp for seven months but had been able to leave because the FBI had been able to establish her loyalty to the United States. She was very hopeful her third attempt to join the WACs would find success, as she was now older and had grown in stature. Unfortunately, the third attempt proved futile, as a heart defect had been found during the required physical and this ended her pursuit.

In January 1944, there were over 120 WACs stationed at Wolters; by March, there were 160.[353] The camp personnel officer, Arthur L. Shumate, praised the WACs, stating, "We wish we had 160 more like the ones we have."[354] The WACs at Wolters were so effective at recruiting and doing their jobs that the Eighth Service Command made Camp Wolters WAC District Headquarters and Enlisting Station for nine surrounding counties in 1944.[355]

The WACs had numerous recruitment drives but decided to try a different tactic in June 1944. They invited the public to come to camp and participate in tours of their facilities. The visitors were driven around in an army vehicle; shown classrooms where WACs were studying the Articles of War; taken to the Reception Center, where most of the WACs worked; shown the barracks and mess hall; and concluded the tour with refreshments in the dayroom of the Reception Center.[356] The success of this recruitment drive was not reported.

In August 1944, it was announced that the Reception Center and Literacy School would close.[357] The Reception Center was closed as part of the army's move to consolidate programs and economize.[358] Inductees continued to be processed at Fort Sam Houston, Fort Bliss or Fort Sill.[359] The Literacy School was closed due to a policy change in how to treat men that were considered illiterate.[360] If illiterate men spoke English and were in good physical and mental condition, they would go into special units, work with construction crews or maintenance units, become stevedores and do other manual labor jobs.[361] The loss of these units was lamented in that week's "The Soldier Is a Gal," column in the camp newspaper, as it meant that many of the WACs would be transferred to other installations.[362] Before any WACs left, they had a final party with all the Reception Center staff on Morrison Hill and dubbed it "the best party the RC has ever had."[363] The remaining WACs did not have long to miss their old friends, as new WACs arrived the next week. The WAC unit 4824 joined the 1866 and took on new positions in various areas of the camp.[364]

The WACs had the smallest canteen at camp. It was an eight-by-eight former linen closet that was converted into their PX.[365] It opened on September 19, 1944, and was only open during the hours of 6:30–9:30 p.m. Sergeant Anne Lorenzo ran the PX; she worked as a dispatcher for the Ordnance Motor Pool during the day. The WACs had the longest wait time of any other detail in getting a PX, as they had already been at camp a year and three months before their PX opened.

Not long after V-E Day, the WACs celebrated their third national birthday, May 15, 1945. They celebrated with a picnic and knew that they might be called overseas at any time. Many had already left for places like the Philippines, Guam, India and countries in Europe. At that point, most of the WACs worked in the hospital or in other medical sections.[366] They were starting another recruitment drive and hoped it would not be long before Japan was defeated.

Their hopes came true, and Japan surrendered on August 14, 1945. Washington called for a stop to WAC recruiting, and demobilization began.[367] WAC director Hobby resigned after V-E Day, and the new director, Lieutenant Colonel Westray Boyce, oversaw the demobilization after V-J Day.[368] While everyone was happy about the war being over, not all the women were happy about losing their jobs. For married women, this was the first time they had been able to get a job away from home, and many enjoyed working and earning their own money. With the war over, and men coming back home, the WACs knew their employment outlook was not good.[369]

It is unclear as to when the WACs left Wolters. According to the camp newspaper, the last "Soldier Is a Gal" column was published on June 1, 1945; three WACs are mentioned on the sports page in the August 3, 1945 issue; and the last mention of Wolters WACs is in the August 31, 1945 issue.[370] It states that released WACs were eligible for job assistance and that the WAC first sergeant left for a new assignment.[371] The WAC program became a permanent part of the army on June 12, 1948. Initially, there had been doubts about their ability to perform their jobs under stressful situations, and often they were written off as "just another pretty face" by soldiers and officers alike who insisted that there was no place for women in the army. Still, the WACs hung in and never gave up, going overseas and performing their duties even when they were under enemy fire. They more than proved their worth to the army, and they proved themselves to be soldiers. After the war, General Eisenhower stated, "During the time I have had WACs under my command they have met every test and task assigned to them....Their contributions in efficiency, skill, spirit and determination are immeasurable."[372]

While the WACs entering the army initially went against the grain of American culture, they were eventually accepted and appreciated, unlike the African American soldiers and as opposed to the POWs, who were imprisoned at Wolters. The POWs were never wanted and hated by most but found some appreciation from local farmers through hard, laborious work. As the possibility of war loomed closer, General Marshall and his staff began preparations. This included what would happen to captured enemy soldiers. General Marshall emphasized to his staff that all prisoners of war (POWs) were to be treated in accordance with the Geneva Conventions of War of 1929. Prisoner of war matters fell to the Provost Marshal General's (PMG) Office, and it started formulating plans at once.[373] At the onset of war, there were not many POWs, and there was not a problem housing them. Following the PMG's plans, unused military camps were utilized until permanent prisoner of war camps could be built. The decision was made to put the permanent prisoner of war camps throughout the Southwest, due to its warmer climate.[374] Many of these camps were under the Eighth Service Command, which fell under the Southern Defense Command.[375]

In August 1942, Great Britain asked the United States for help in housing the POWs it had taken.[376] The United States agreed but needed time to get facilities ready to house the 150,000 POWs that Great Britain wanted to send.[377] By the time the POWs started arriving in late 1942/early 1943, the United States was taking more Axis prisoners itself from North Africa. The number of POWs held in the United States in August 1942 was 65; by August 1943, it was 130,299.[378] That number would keep on growing until it peaked at 425,871 in May 1945.[379] The dramatic increase in prisoners called for some creative thinking on the part of the PMG's Office and the Eighth Service Command.

The Eighth Service Command announced on November 12, 1943, that German and Italian POWs who had been at permanent prisoner

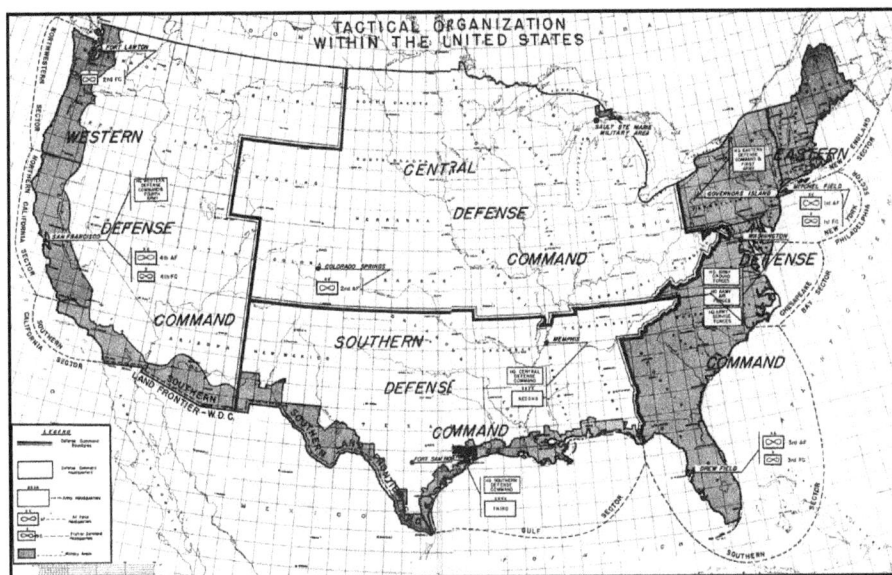

A map of various Service Commands in the continental United States, 1942. In 1942, the Eighth Service Command consisted of Texas, Louisiana, Arkansas, New Mexico and Oklahoma and fell under the Southern Defense Command. *From https://texaspowerwagon. com/8th-Svc-Cmd.htm.*

camps were being moved to various military posts throughout the Eighth Command district to be used as temporary laborers. There was a labor shortage at this time, especially in agriculture, and the POWs were to be used to fill this shortage. One of the many camps chosen to house POWs temporarily was Camp Wolters.[380] The POWs did various kinds of labor: painting, agricultural work, maintenance, carpentry and such. They were paid eighty cents a day for their work and bought items from the PX with this money. The camp paper initially predicted five hundred prisoners at the site, noting that while Italian prisoners had given their previous guards no problem, German prisoners had been "tough customers— haughty and cocky."[381]

The actual date that the POWs started to arrive at Wolters is in question. Some internet articles suggest that they arrived as early as 1942, which is inaccurate considering the announcement of the Eighth Service Command that was made in late 1943 (as previously noted). A former deputy commander of the camp, Colonel Willie H. Casper Jr. (see endnote 382) has research indicating that German POWs were at Wolters from 1943 to 1945.[382] The October 22, 1943 edition of the camp newspaper says the POWs are coming but doesn't mention a possible arrival date. Nothing is mentioned of the POWs being at Wolters in the camp newspaper until the June 23, 1944 edition.[383] A search of regional newspapers from 1943 to 1944 and the *Texas Almanacs* for those years also did not turn up any information on a more specific date. The only certainty is that at some point between October 22, 1943, and June 23, 1944, Axis POWs arrived at Wolters.[384]

According to Casper, the vast majority of POWs at Wolters were Germans, most taken in North Africa.[385] They were housed in the old Camp Wolters buildings that had been constructed by the Civilian Conservation Corps in the 1930s. Additionally, the army had to erect temporary buildings constructed of "heavy tarpaper over pine frames with sheetrock interiors" to house all the POWs.[386] Casper states that there were three hundred POWs, not the five hundred as reported in the camp newspaper.[387] The total enclosure was 600 feet by 2,500 feet and was surrounded with a double fence of barbed wire. The inside fence was 8 feet high, and the outer fence was 10 feet high with twenty-one strands of barbed wire at the top; there was 6 feet between fences. The barbed wire was attached to iron rods that angled inward and included trip alarm wires. Each corner of the enclosure had a sentry tower and floodlights were operated at night.[388]

Within this enclosure was an administrative building for management of the POWs, a chapel, nineteen barracks, two mess halls, a kitchen and a recreational area.[389] The chapel was a part of a recreation room. The barracks were forty by eighty feet and slept fifty POWs. The POWs slept on folding metal cots covered with straw mattresses. The POWs painted some murals on these walls and in the mess halls. They were able to have a radio, receive mail and packages and send mail. The mess halls were made of two converted barracks. Their tables seated eight and were in rows; they were fed three meals a day. The kitchen was between the two mess halls and had a serving line for each mess hall. Their clothes were laundered in the Camp Wolters laundry, where some of them worked. Their outside recreation area was two hundred by five hundred feet, and they could play basketball, volleyball, soccer, croquet, horseshoes or tennis. Inside they could play bingo, cards, dominoes, backgammon or checkers.[390]

There were two diets for the prisoners, one for those who had active work duties and one for those who did not work. Active workers got three thousand calories a day, while those who did not work got two thousand calories a day.[391] Some of the prisoners did not like their American food and refused to eat it. This led to food waste. The PMG's Office chose

...Art By German POWs

Mural from POW mess hall.
Courtesy Willie H. Casper Jr.,
Pictorial History of Fort Wolters,
vol. 1, Infantry Replacement
Training Center, *1940, Boyce Ditto*
Library, Special Collections.

to solve this problem by lowering the daily calorie intake by five hundred calories and closing the canteen during meals. The POWs grumbled about this, and the Red Cross was called in to investigate. The food was considered good but of limited quantity. The calorie intake was increased by two hundred calories a day. A strike was threatened by the prisoners, but no actions were taken.[392]

When outside of their enclosure, POWs wore blue work coveralls with a large "PW" sewn onto the front and back. In the enclosure, they could wear their uniforms or khaki pants and a shirt with a P on the left sleeve and a W on the right sleeve.[393] In May 1945, the army had to issue a warning to the citizens of Mineral Wells and surrounding area that if they were caught wearing clothing with PW written on it and failed to halt when told to do so, they could be shot. It had become somewhat of a joke that the "high school students and other civilians" would paint PW on their clothes and run through town. Only POWs were to wear clothing with PW written on them, and the army wanted to emphasize how unsafe this joke could be.[394]

There were not many discipline problems with the prisoners. The prisoners policed themselves and "often lived in fear of their fellow prisoners [more] than their captors."[395] However, there were a handful of times when problems did arise. The most serious occurred in July 1945, when around seventy prisoners decided that it was too hot to work outside and refused to work. There were too many to put in the guardhouse, so the commander had a small fenced compound made for them. He put them on bread and water and forced them to work at hard labor for two weeks. When their time was up, they no longer complained about the weather conditions.

Casper describes the process of hiring out POWs to work in the community on page 91 of his book *Pictorial History of Fort Wolters*, volume 1, *Infantry Replacement Training Center*. Local businessmen and farmers could request that POWs work at their businesses or farms if the person making the request agreed to the terms of the Geneva Convention and provided protection for the POWs. Prisoners had the option to choose if they wanted to work outside the enclosure or not, but most agreed. At Camp Wolters, most of those who requested POW workers were ranchers and farmers. They could request two to twenty-five workers. If more than ten were requested, a guard had to accompany them. The POWs were used mostly for agricultural work, working with farm animals, building farm buildings and mending fences. The employer fed the POWs lunch and, sometimes, gave them cigarettes and "home brews." Casper states that their pay ranged from seventy-five cents to one dollar. This contrasts with the eighty cents reported by George Lewis and John Mewha.[396] Their pay was exchanged for coupons that could be used at the canteen to purchase food or personal items. What money was left over was put into an account in their name at the Camp Controller's Office. When the war was over, they collected their money, which had accrued interest.[397]

By March 1944, there were 183,618 POWs in the United States.[398] Their labor was of high importance to the agricultural industry, where they were used in the fields. They also did maintenance work around the camps.

There were only two reported incidences of Wolters' POWs running away from their place of employment.[399] The first time two POWs went missing was July 11, 1944; they fled from Burrus Mills, where they had been working. They were last seen unloading grain at the mill. When the truck from camp came to get the prisoners at the end of the day, neither were there. A search was started for them.[400] Casper reports that they both returned within a few days, as the POWs realized they had no money, they did not know the language and their "survival was questionable."[401]

The other time was March 20, 1945, when two prisoners disappeared from camp. The POWs were Alfred Runge and Karl-Heinz Huth, both of whom spoke English. They were captured on March 22 in Bennett, Texas, sleeping near a brickyard.[402] Mr. and Mrs. R.C. Nall saw the prisoners taking baths and notified police. They had maps of South Texas and Mexico and food in their possession.[403] They were arrested and returned to Wolters.[404]

In February 1945, Major Kolbein Johnson, who had been commander of the POW camp at Wolters, was transferred, and Captain Clayton H. Erskine took over. He had previously worked at the POW camp at Fort Russell.[405]

Chaplain John G. Elser, a Lutheran minister who spoke German, became chaplain to the POWs at Wolters.[406] He conducted the funeral for three POWs who were accidentally killed on September 21, 1945, in an explosion at the salvage yard on base.[407] Two American soldiers and three other

POWs were injured in the blast. The POWs were buried close to the POW compound. Three hearses and the other POWs accompanied the bodies to the cemetery. An American squad fired three rounds for the dead.[408] Casper states that the cemetery was five hundred yards east of the Mineral Wells High School, as it stood at the time.[409] The cemetery was enclosed by a rock wall the prisoners built.

Casper states that seven POWs died at Wolters.[410] From information he found at the National War Museum, he lists the three discussed in the previous paragraph as being Alfred Daries, Heinrich Bobo and Werner Goetz. A prisoner named Martin Karebeck was killed on April 23, 1944, when he was working at a ranch.[411] A woman is listed as being buried in the POW cemetery, though no woman is on record as being a POW. The woman is known as Mildred Morie Schulls; she died on September 26, 1945, but no cause of death is listed.[412] Local residents stated that three POWs died of pneumonia, but no record of their deaths has been found.[413] After the war, four POW bodies were flown back to Germany, and three were left unclaimed. Their remains were transferred to Camp Bowie, Texas.

When the war was over, POWs were quickly sent back to their home countries. In January 1945, there was an estimated 41,455 POWs in Texas; by January 1, 1946, the number was down to 23,967.[414] With the majority of POWs gone, the POW camp at Wolters closed on April 5, 1946, and the few POWs that were left were shipped to Camp Bowie.[415]

In 1991, Ed Dombrowsky, a former German POW who had been kept at Wolters, returned to Mineral Wells. He was seeking the grave of his friend who had died in the salvage yard explosion.[416] Dombrowsky was unable to locate the cemetery but made friends with a local man, Cecil Ward, who knew the old camp's area. Dombrowsky showed Ward where the "huts" they stayed in as POWs were located and where other POW buildings had been. Dombrowsky had been twenty-one years old when he left Wolters. After the war, he moved to Canada and was still living there at the time of his visit.

None of the groups discussed in this chapter had an easy time during the war, but their efforts were rewarded in the long run. President Truman ended segregation in the army in 1948, and the following war, the Korean War, saw all races of soldiers in the same units. The WACs continued to be a separate group within the army until 1978, when they became integrated with the regular army. In 2016, they were allowed to hold any position within the army, including combat units. The German POWs went back to their homeland, which had been destroyed and subsequently divided between the west and east at Berlin. It is not known what happened to the German POWs at Wolters, except for Dombrowsky; however, their time in the United States would have provided them with a life-changing experience that would be hard to forget.

Chapter 5

ECONOMIC IMPACT

W hile the army focused on getting the soldiers trained for combat, the city of Mineral Wells focused on making sure the soldiers made the most of their free time. The city hosted every kind of entertainment imaginable, from parades to wolf hunts; if a soldier thought of something he wanted to do, the city did its best to provide it. The *Dallas Morning News* wrote an article about Mineral Wells in June 1941, which glowingly said, "No Army town could be approaching the problem of providing recreation for these homesick kids with more zest than Mineral Wells."[417] Mineral Wells was becoming the place to be and started making record-breaking financial gains, but a myriad of problems came along with this economic boost, problems that other military towns across the nation also faced, such as major housing shortages, increased crime, health and safety issues, overburdening of the school system and traffic troubles. Mineral Wells faced all these challenges and many more during its time as home to an active World War II army camp but would find that its efforts readily paid off with short-term economic gains and long-term infrastructure investments.

The *Dallas Morning News* June 1941 article previously referenced detailed the lengths to which the town had gone to get a recreation center for the soldiers. Private donations had allowed the local Defense Recreation Council chairman, Harold Dennis, to rent two floors above a Safeway grocery store to use as the recreation center; this became home to the first USO.[418] Equipment for the center came from old WPA recreation halls and private citizens, who donated tables, chairs, a piano, games of all types and even

North Oak
USO 1940s
postcard. This
was the main
USO building
in Mineral
Wells. *Author's
personal collection.*

their own furniture. Dennis was quick to remind people that the current recreation center was temporary. The town had applied for funding from the Federal Security Agency to build a brand-new building in the near future. The city had already donated a two-hundred-by-four-hundred-foot lot in the downtown area to be used for the new building.

Funds in the amount of $77,500 for the recreation center were approved in October 1941 by the WPA Defense Project.[419] Bids were submitted, and the former site of the Standard Pavilion on North Oak became a construction site.[420] The new USO building officially opened on March 15, 1942.[421] It was located at 607 North Oak Street. It had "a large auditorium, lounges, reading and writing rooms, telephones, soda fountain, ping-pong tables, radios, pianos, newspapers and magazines."[422] There were weekly dances on Saturday nights, bingo parties, musicals and occasionally special entertainment. This was not the only USO in Mineral Wells; there was a total of five, and the city boasted about them all. The USO located at 200 West Hubbard was run by the National Catholic Community Service.[423] It had many of the same features as the main club but also contained recording machines for the soldiers to make special recordings for their families. They also had Saturday night dances, community sings, party nights and movie nights and always provided refreshments. The club located at 316 Southeast First Street was a women's center. It was run by the USO for the soldiers' wives. Women could turn here for entertainment but also found help getting jobs and finding housing as well as just to receive support from other army wives. The club at Southeast Sixth Avenue and Fourteenth Street was for noncommissioned officers and opened on January 10, 1942. This was the first club of its kind for noncommissioned officers.[424] There were three thousand noncoms assigned to Wolters, and over five hundred were married with children. It had similar accommodations as the main USO club on

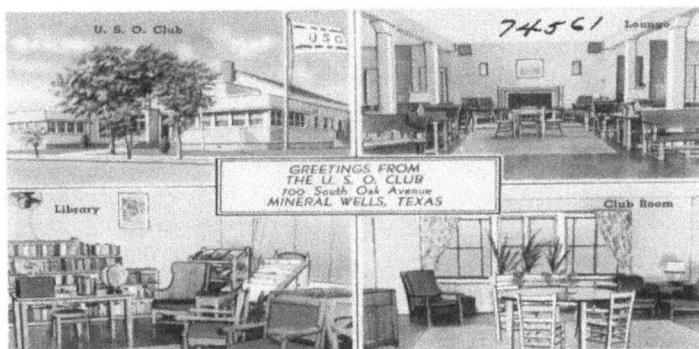

The African American USO in Mineral Wells; it later became a community center. *From https://www.digitalcommonwealth.org/search/commonwealth:zk51w184h.*

North Oak, as did the "Colored USO Club," located at 700 South Oak.[425] The "Colored USO" opened the afternoon of October 5, 1941, with entertainment provided by soldiers from the camp.[426]

The nationally known Baker Hotel opened its pool nightly for use by the trainees, and the local country club allowed the men to play a round of golf on their eighteen-hole course, clubs and balls included, for fifty cents. The town purchased lights for the softball and baseball fields so that trainees could play after dark. If none of this activity appealed to the trainees, there were also two bowling alleys and five movie theaters. On Sunday afternoons, citizens volunteered to take the trainees on scenic tours of the county, and one rancher even volunteered to take some on a wolf hunt.[427] While Mineral Wells certainly rolled out the red carpet for the white soldiers, this was still the segregated South. None of the mentioned activities or places, besides the "Colored USO," were open to the African American troops. The African American newspaper the *Chicago Defender* does discuss some activities for the African American troops.

In addition to the USO clubs, the soldiers were allowed to use the Convention Hall on North Oak Avenue. Here they had variety shows on Tuesdays, folk and square-dancing classes on Thursday and weekly Saturday night dances. The Mineral Wells Convention Hall also offered a basketball court, a stage, badminton and volleyball courts.[428]

Officers of Camp Wolters, members of the Mineral Wells Chamber of Commerce and officials from the American Legion planned the first Army Day celebration with Camp Wolters for April 7, 1941. This first celebration welcomed the new commander, Brigadier General Simpson, and his wife. The day included a parade, an inspection by the public of soldier drills, a formal troop retreat, a tour of the camp and night entertainment, including a free amateur show and dance at the Convention Hall for the enlisted

Top: Mineral Wells Convention
Hall, Mineral Wells, Texas.
Mineral Wells was a popular site
for conventions before the war.
Author's personal collection.

Middle: Women waiting for the
dancing to begin. *Courtesy* Fort
Worth Star-Telegram *Collection,
May 30, 1941, Special Collections,
University of Texas at Arlington
Libraries.*

Bottom: This photo is of the
lobby of the Camp Wolters
Housing Office. *Courtesy* Fort
Worth Star-Telegram *Collection,
January 5, 1945, Special Collection,
University of Texas at Arlington.*

men.[429] Army Day celebrations became a yearly fixture throughout the war and were a way to get the community behind the war effort.

Music from live bands and orchestras could be heard every weekend as dances were held at multiple locations throughout the town. To ensure that the men had someone to dance with, a master index file was created listing hundreds of women that would be willing to attend and dance with the soldiers. There was 1 chaperone for every 8 "girls," and a girl could not get in unless she had a special card.[430] To ensure a partner for the Saturday night dance, a soldier signed up by Thursday to receive a ticket that he pinned to his coat for admission.[431] It was estimated that there were 4 soldiers for every female. The biggest dance held at the camp was the New Year's Eve Dance of 1944, at the Sports Arena. That night, the Sports Arena held 3,500 soldiers and their dates. Five busloads of women came from Fort Worth and the surrounding areas to ensure everyone had a partner to dance with. Lines formed around the building, and couples were seen dancing outside in the streets.[432]

Along with all this entertainment came a few problems. The largest problem faced by Mineral Wells and military towns throughout the nation was the problem of housing. Most military towns were not equipped to deal with the onslaught of people that came with the army; not even a town that billed itself as "the South's greatest health resort" could house the families and visitors of over twenty thousand men.[433] Add in the number of workers needed to take care of such a large amount of people, and Mineral Wells was bursting at the seams.[434]

The men and families of Camp Wolters did receive some help in finding living quarters through the Camp Wolters Housing Office. This was one of the few Camp Wolters offices not located at the actual camp. It was on the second floor of the post office in Mineral Wells, and a smaller office was located at the chamber of commerce in Weatherford. Families were discouraged from coming to visit for more than a weekend, and arrangements had to be made far in advance and approved by the housing officer, Captain W.E. Davis.[435] Local hotels filled up rapidly on weekends and holidays. Rental prices for rooms and houses were approved by the Housing Office before occupancy, and a form had to be filled out within twenty-four hours of vacancy.[436] Later, in May 1942, a private organization, Army Emergency Relief Incorporated, opened to help army families with various problems, including housing.[437]

If you were a civilian, with or without a family, there were not many places to turn to for help. The Red Cross served meals to some, but they mostly worked with the army and their families. Even workers who originally had a place to live were turned away by their landlords because they were not able to pay the newly increased rents. The strike by food workers in February 1941, demanding a wage increase because they could no longer afford to pay rent with their current salaries, demonstrates how the lack of adequate housing affected everyone, not just the military.[438]

Officials from Washington visited with General Simpson, his staff, Mineral Wells mayor John Miller and the Army Advisory Board during the week of May 5, 1941. The problem with housing had become so severe that without more living quarters, many officers were being forced to move to surrounding towns.[439] In fact, Weatherford, a neighboring town about eighteen miles east of the camp, was already building new homes for the incoming military families.[440] In May 1941, FDR approved a defense housing program that would bring one hundred new homes to Camp Wolters families. Each home was to cost no more than $3,500 as set by law.[441]

The Houston Redy-Cut House Company received a contract from Camp Wolters for one hundred prefabricated homes. These were for the noncommissioned officers and civilian employees of the camp. The houses were completed within sixty days.[442] On August 29, the Federal Works administrator, John M. Carmody, approved and named the defense housing projects for Camp Wolters. The Elmhurst Park project would house eighty-five families of white soldiers. The Huachuca Place project would house fifteen African American families.[443] On November 29, 1941, the housing officer announced that one hundred new houses were available for buying or leasing by application. By the end of that day, 303 people had already applied.[444] These housing projects helped only a small fraction of the people that needed housing. By January 1942, 2,000 of the Camp Wolters' permanent cadre lived outside of the camp.[445] Housing became one of the most persistent problems that the army and other military towns faced throughout the war.

To assist with the housing problem, Washington created a section within the Price Administration and Civilian Supply (PACS) Department specifically for housing issues. In some military towns, landlords had more than doubled the price for rent, which placed the rental property out of reach for the common soldier or everyday civilian worker. Frank C. Ralls was the senior field representative for the Rent Section of PACS and investigated the housing situation in Mineral Wells and Weatherford for several days in August 1941. After speaking with General Simpson and the Committee on Fair Housing and Rent, Ralls concluded that Mineral Wells had everything well in hand. He said, "The fact that rentals have been reduced to a fair level in Mineral Wells and Weatherford, except for a few isolated cases, evidences a close co-operation between the Army, the citizens, the Chamber of Commerce, city, county, and school district officials."[446] He further stated that "the plan adopted by General Simpson to handle the rent situation in the Mineral Wells area shows that voluntary efforts produce results." General Simpson and his committee members worked out a plan; the camp housing officer and a public inspector would inspect the proposed rental property, talk with the owner and together agree on a fair rental price. If an agreement could not be reached, then the case was taken to a subcommittee of the Fair Housing and Rent Control Board. There, each party would present their side and, with the help of the subcommittee, come up with an agreed-on price.[447] Subsequent research based on oral history suggests that the "voluntary" control perhaps included intimidation by a citizens committee.[448] Despite these measures, a lack of supply meant that rents continued to rise. Between September 1941 and January 1942, rent in Mineral Wells increased 46 percent.[449] The average rate for a three-bedroom furnished apartment, with all bills paid, was thirty to thirty-five dollars a month. The average rate for a four-bedroom, unfurnished house was forty dollars per month.[450] In June 1942, the government stepped in again and threatened maximum rents would be fixed as of January 1943, and this meant that landlords had to go back to the price they were charging on January 1, 1941.[451] This did not happen, as many of the landlords and public officials agreed to a rent reduction. However, a rent attorney, Homer Bouldin, was appointed for the Camp Wolters area, who began strict enforcement of rent controls for Palo Pinto–Parker area.[452] Bouldin was also president of the Mineral Wells Chamber of Commerce.

In addition to the families of commissioned officers moving to town, it was estimated that as many as four hundred families of noncommissioned officers made Mineral Wells their new home. Not only did this add to the housing problem, but it also placed stress on the school system. The Mineral Wells superintendent went to Washington in the fall of 1941 to ask for help with the dramatic increase in students. Mineral Wells had a total scholastic population of 1,710 students for the 1940–41 school year; for the 1941–42 school year, that number increased to 2,511, an increase of 46.8 percent.[453] Schools throughout the country were dealing with the same issue wherever military camps had been built. The schools had no money to accommodate all the new students, and school districts desperately needed assistance. Congress interceded and passed legislation that helped school districts in defense areas with $115 million in additional funds.[454] The Mineral Wells schools were awarded an initial grant of $518,390 by the Federal Works Agency for school improvements in November 1941.[455] Mineral Wells Independent School District passed a school bond of $70,000 early in 1942 and started building new schools right away. The government added $503,000 to the expansion.[456] Later, in 1944, the Federal Works Agency gave $10,884 to Mineral Wells for additional school facilities.[457] By 1944, Camp Wolters had increased the overall estimated population of Mineral Wells by 114.8 percent.[458] Mineral Wells was also able to spend more money per student as funding increased. In 1940–41, Mineral Wells spent $32.98 per white student and $15.60 per African American student. In 1945–46, it spent $59.53 on white students, an increase of 80.5 percent, and $35.32 per African American student, or an increase of 126.4 percent.[459]

As previously stated, there were continuous problems with water, sewage and traffic. Initially, the base started with a new water treatment plant, settling basins and pumping units to bring the more than two million gallons of water per day from Lake Mineral Wells to the camp.[460] However, by the fall of 1941, the city was once again looking to enlarge its water system. A dual water line was installed running from Lake Mineral Wells to the camp, and the system was enlarged with a grant of $211,000 from the government combined with a $26,000 loan by the city.[461] These improvements still did not meet the demand of the city and camp. In February 1942, it was announced that the Federal Works Agency would supply the bulk of $402,000 in water and sewer upgrades that were needed.[462] When the work was finished in April 1944, the city had the capacity to carry six million gallons of water per day.[463] The hot Texas summers also caused problems. The over one-hundred-degree temperatures and lack of rain frequently brought drought conditions and forced water restrictions during the summer months.[464]

The water and sewage issues were problematic, but they were not deadly like the traffic problems were. State troopers increased patrols on US 80 from Weatherford to Mineral Wells, and the camp newspapers warned soldiers that the speed limit of thirty-five miles per hour would be strictly enforced.[465] However, traffic problems were part of a national problem for all cities that had a military base or defense manufacturing. In 1941, the Texas Public Safety Department recorded "13 accidents, 6 deaths, and 12 major injuries in six-weeks on a three-mile segment of US 80" from the eastern Mineral Wells city limits to the entrance of Camp Wolters. Government agencies collaborated on a plan to reduce this problem and publicized their efforts. On this same three-mile segment, traffic officers switched from cars to motorcycles; warning signs were posted at both entrances to the camp.

A walkway was put in that went from the camp to the city, and no parking was allowed from the middle of Mineral Wells to the eastern city limit. City traffic lights were operated manually during shift changes, highway patrol schedules were changed that coincided with peak times of congestion. More arrests were made when accidents occurred. The plan proved very successful. For the next forty-three weeks after implementation, there were "only five accidents, one death, and five injuries." This plan was then adapted and applied to other military sites throughout Texas and the country.[466]

Among the many problems military towns faced was increased criminal activity. Palo Pinto was a "dry" county, and the only legal way of obtaining liquor was with a doctor's prescription. However, many workers and soldiers found a way around that requirement, and when inebriated, they sometimes participated in unlawful activities that kept the police and sheriff busy. The Mineral Wells police arrested twenty-seven men over the weekend of April 12–13, 1941, for excessive drinking and dice playing. Most alarming for the police was when they arrested two Camp Wolters soldiers for robbing a man of eighty-five dollars and were held at the city jail.[467] The police "arrested thirty men" on Sunday, May 31, 1941, for various crimes, including public intoxication, gambling, shooting craps and carrying a concealed weapon.[468] Crime statistics for this time period are not available through the Palo Pinto County Clerk or District Clerk's offices. The county weekly newspaper, the *Palo Pinto County Star*, often printed information about arrests and incidents that happened the previous week which involved the police or sheriff's offices, and larger city newspapers, such as the *Fort Worth Star-Telegram* and the *Dallas Morning News* often printed these stories as well.[469] From the numerous newspaper articles printed about events that included law enforcement activity in Mineral Wells, one can conclude that criminal activity was not slowing down during the army's stay at Mineral Wells.

A health issue that plagued many military towns and the army was sexually transmitted diseases. Prostitution and venereal disease are problems that come with war. It was not a new problem to the army, as George Washington had to deal with these same issues during the Revolutionary War.[470] Gus Blass, a trainee at Wolters during the summer of 1942, joked that "some of the boys called Mineral Wells 'Venereal Wells.'"[471] Two of the army camps in North Texas had seen an increase in this problem due to "camp followers" or prostitutes. Camp Bowie and Camp Barkeley had reported travel trailers parked along the roads at night with women inviting men to stop for a visit. This problem gave rise to an increase in selectees visiting the camp medical units and caused men to fall behind in their training schedules. Abilene, where Camp Barkeley was located, began a clinic for prostitutes and stepped-up arrests. Brownwood, where Camp Bowie was located, increased arrests and fines for vagrancy.[472] General Simpson, of Camp Wolters, addressed community leaders on April 14, 1941, and assured them that Camp Wolters did not have this problem. He said that he did not expect this to be a problem until the camp reached capacity in June and would address the issue immediately when that happened. Each of the six areas of the camp had a prophylaxis station in its dispensary. Here, trainees could pick up information before a night on the town and be reminded that they were to seek treatment within two hours of exposure.[473]

Mayor John C. Miller and Mineral Wells chief of police Frank Granbury "ordered questionable women out of the city." The cities of Abilene and Sweetwater issued similar warnings.[474] A new campaign to clean up Mineral Wells sponsored by the army, city, county and state health authorities; the police and sheriff's department; the district attorney; the county judge; and the liquor control board began the week of October 6, 1941. This campaign was not aimed at people picking up their garbage; rather, it was a campaign for them to clean up their morals. The army named twenty establishments as being "off limits" to the soldiers. These included cafés, bars and dance halls. These places were patrolled by MPs and city police. The campaign also wanted to clean up "diseased women." "All women found in the city with venereal disease were to be locked up and put under treatment until cured."[475] The campaign to clean up Mineral Wells made progress. It was reported the weekend of October 11–12, 1941, ten women having venereal disease were locked up and charged with vagrancy.[476] On October 16, 1941, the sponsors inspected various establishments and placed twelve more establishments on the "off limits" list. The list now contained thirty to thirty-five establishments that soldiers could not visit. This time, the sponsors had looked at the actual cleanliness of the establishments, trash in alleyways and such. The committee members told establishment owners to clean up or risk losing soldiers' business for good.[477] This campaign did seem to work; a headline from a July 1942 *Fort Worth Star-Telegram* article read, "Camp Wolters Has Less Social Disease."[478] The article also gave credit to the May Act, which was passed in June 1941, that gave local authorities more control over "vice in areas near military establishments."[479] In 1944, the state health department's Rapid Treatment Center in Mineral Wells was slated to become one of seven venereal hospitals in Texas. These hospitals were a "war-time measure" that quickly treated infectious diseases of all kinds. They offered to "treat prostitutes and promiscuous women found to be infected."[480] By May 1944, the hospitals were deemed a success, and by the end of June, Washington was giving them more money so the hospitals could be expanded.[481] By 1946 and 1947, venereal disease was under control with a reported sixty-one cases in 1946, the last year Camp Wolters was open, and a low of only twenty-two cases in 1947, a year after the camp closed.[482]

Camp Wolters did adversely affect the spa and convention business. Mineral Wells was well known for the healing properties of its mineral waters, and many people traveled from all over to "take the cure" by drinking or bathing in these famed mineral waters. When the army moved in, the bathers and health seekers did not come back. It has been speculated that many bathers feared they would not be able to find comfortable lodging. While the hotels and boardinghouses did not suffer any loss in business, some owners did state that the bathing business decreased by at least 50 percent.[483] Mineral Wells, also well known for having conventions, was forced to cancel or reschedule some of the conventions in 1942 because of the housing shortage. Convention planners often decided to relocate conventions, fearing there would not be enough housing or eating facilities to accommodate their attendees because of the number of visitors Camp Wolters regularly pulled in. One of these conventions was the American Legion of Texas convention, which, held prior to the war, brought several thousand attendees to town.[484]

The city and county did thrive having the camp in Mineral Wells. The county banks had shown a great deal of growth between 1940 and 1941, as an analysis of deposits from March 1, 1941, to the previous year's deposits (deposit totals on March 1, 1940). The two banks of Mineral Wells showed the largest increases. The State Bank had deposits of $1,043,384.25 in 1940 and deposits of $1,658,823.47 in 1941, a 62.8 percent growth. The City National Bank had deposits of $972,461.52 in 1940 and deposits of 1,376,233.89 in 1941, a 70.6 percent growth, but this was just the beginning.[485] The 1946 statement of the City National Bank showed deposits of $4,240,348.00, and the State National Bank showed $4,012,508.00.[486] The deposits of both banks combined—$3,035,057.00 in 1941 to the 1946 deposits, $8,252,856.00—indicate an increase of 171.9 percent.

Along with income, the town's infrastructure also grew. With the increased military traffic, the Civil Aeronautics Authority (CAA) decided that Mineral Wells needed a larger airport, costing $300,000. The district airport engineer, J.D. Church, surveyed a proposed area on July 26, 1941. The CAA needed room enough for runways 1 mile long and 500 feet wide. Facilities included a weather observatory, beacons and lighted fields.[487] Construction began in

September 1942 and included two runways, each 4,500 feet long. Total costs were estimated at $579,000.[488] By 1946, the Mineral Wells Airport was rated a Class Three field, had four runways and was home to Pioneer Airlines, which flew six flights per day and serviced fourteen Texas cities.[489]

A larger infrastructure supported an increase in manufacturing and related businesses. In 1941, Palo Pinto County had fourteen manufacturing companies, employing 141 people, with wages totaling $104,710.[490] In 1943, W.W. Bateman opened a steel plant that would remain in operation until the end of the century; in June 1945, the Jaques Power Saw Company opened an eleven-acre steel yard; and in August 1945, the McGaugh Hoisery and Manufacturing Company signed papers to open a hosiery mill.[491] In 1947, the year after the camp closed, Palo Pinto County reported nineteen manufacturing companies employing 358 employees, with wages totaling $695,000 or an increase of 563.7 percent.[492] During the same time period (1941–46), the county saw a change in county retail receipts from $4,171,000 to $6,843,000, or an increase of 64 percent.[493] The county income increased from $7,893,000 to $14,078,000, or 78.3 percent.[494] Houses increased countywide from 5,599 in 1940 to 6,490 in 1950, or 15.9 percent, with the largest increase in Mineral Wells (from 1,932 to 3,089, or 59.8 percent).[495] Southwestern Bell Telephone service increased connections from 1,850 in 1940 to 2, 964 in 1945, or 60 percent.[496] Population in the county went from 18,456 to 20,000, or 8.3 percent.[497] Mineral Wells' population went from 6,303 to 11,000, or 74.5 percent.[498] Marriages increased from 191 in 1940 to 490 in 1945, or 157 percent, and births increased from 351 in 1940 to 580 in 1945, or 65 percent.[499]

Mineral Wells made quite an impression on many of the army wives. An article entitled "Mineral Wells Pleasant 'Home in Texas' for Wives of Army Officers" interviewed several army wives living in the Baker Hotel. The wives praised the town, the facilities of the hotel, the local USO (that cared for army children twice a week) and the "ability to go outside almost every day, even in winter."[500] The wives had lived in other army towns before, some even in Texas, but said they had "never had a town open their hearts to us like this town has."[501]

Mineral Wells encountered a number of problems when the army arrived, including severe housing shortages and problems with sanitation, water, traffic, school overcrowding, health issues and criminal activity. Nevertheless, the city took each problem in turn, and with generous financial help from the federal government, it managed to conquer each one, except the housing shortage. The housing shortage did not let up until after V-E Day; then there was plenty of housing, which in turn ended up helping the citizens of Mineral Wells by letting those who had been confined to small rooms and boardinghouses have a chance to buy or rent a one-family home with room for the whole family. The population increased, new businesses opened and economic gains were substantial. The army and Mineral Wells had worked well together, and this experience would lay the foundation for additional growth in the future.

EPILOGUE

C amp Wolters played a vital role in the defense of this country during World War II and, at the same time, transformed the small town of Mineral Wells into a thriving and bustling city with a promising future. The army brought significant and rapid growth to Mineral Wells. The population of the town exploded overnight. When the army arrived in November 1940, Mineral Wells had a resident population of 6,303, but within two months, the city had welcomed a legion of construction workers numbering 18,000. By 1945, the city had a resident population of 11,000. The camp also led to widespread economic growth for Mineral Wells and the county, but it caused multiple problems too. Nevertheless, Mineral Wells handled every problem that it faced and benefited from the results.

The partnership that the army and Mineral Wells forged during this time would bring them back together again and again. The army left Camp Wolters and Mineral Wells in August 1946 but returned in 1951 for the Korean War. This time, Camp Wolters became known as Wolters Air Force Base, a SCARWAF (Special Category Army Reassigned with the Air Force) facility. Then in 1956, the army would take back Wolters and made it into Fort Wolters, the army's primary helicopter training school for the Vietnam War. Fort Wolters closed for good in 1975. Had it not been for this initial partnership during World War II, Mineral Wells may not have had these additional opportunities that continued to cause the city to grow for decades.

The area that Camp Wolters covered is now dotted with various businesses, some homes, a church, cattle and a few remains testifying to its past. A

The only remaining building from Camp Wolters when it was a training camp for the Texas National Guard. *From https://www.waymarking.com/gallery/image. aspx?f=1&guid=d7765e05-692a-45d2-a257-5b2cdf1ba5bf.*

private prison bought some of the land, upgraded the barracks, fenced off the area and held nonviolent prisoners for several years. It is now closed. There is one remaining brick building left from the National Guard days; it sits on the campus of Mineral Wells High School, now designated with a historical marker. It was also a building that housed POWs during World War II. The Texas National Guard still has a presence at the camp, though greatly reduced.

A group of historically minded citizens formed the Fort Wolters Gate Committee and returned the entrance of Fort Wolters to how it looked during the Vietnam era. They also built a memorial to those soldiers who trained at Wolters who had been awarded the Medal of Honor. The committee came together and built the National Vietnam War Museum, which had its grand opening in June 2022.

Mineral Wells is in a state of revival now. Restoration of many of the old buildings and interest in the past are flourishing. New investors are building housing additions across the county and opening new businesses in anticipation of the tourists that they hope will come to see the reopened hotels and many historical venues. The newly opened dance hall in the heart of downtown may not be packing the soldiers in on Saturday night like the ones in the past did, but the memory still lingers. The current Chamber of Commerce members are just as active as those members from 1940, who actively sought to bring Camp Wolters to Mineral Wells and where this story began. By looking to its past, the city is looking for a new beginning, and that story is waiting to unfold.

NOTES

Introduction

1. Texas Historical Commission, Texas Time Travel website, World War II theme, https://www.thc.texas.gov/preserve/projects-and-programs/military-sites/texas-world-war-ii.

2. Samuel D. Farris, "The Camp Swift Years in Bastrop, Texas: A Rural Community's Social and Economic Transition into an Urban Military Center" (MA thesis, University of Texas at Pan American University, 2007).

3. *The Texas Almanac 1941–1942* (Dallas: A.H. Belo, 1941), 493; *The Texas Almanac 1947–1948* (Dallas: A.H. Belo, 1952), 507; *Texas Almanac 1939–1940* (Dallas: A.H. Belo, 1941), 386; *The Texas Almanac 1945–1946* (Dallas, Texas: A.H. Belo, 1952), 489 (all *Texas Almanacs* accessed through Portal to Texas History, https://texashistory.unt.edu/). *Income* as defined by the *Texas Almanac 1939–1940* means "the sum of individual incomes of all people of county named." The almanac further states, "The figure on income is from Sales Management....This magazine, which is widely accepted as a market authority, bases its estimates of county income on income tax returns, retail sales, and similar factors" (494).

4. "City's Bond Indebtedness Is Reduced, Water Works Bond Now Around $417,000," *Mineral Wells Index*, February 20, 1946, 1, accessed through Portal to Texas History, https://texashistory.unt.edu/; "U.S.O. Plans New Centers in Mineral Wells," *Palo Pinto County Star*, October 24, 1941, 1; "Federal Funds OK'd for 2 Schools in Texas," *Dallas Morning*

News, March 17, 1944, 2, Infoweb-Newsbank.com. The new home sales number comes from the difference between dwelling units reported in 1940 and those reported for 1950 (*Texas Almanac 1952–53*, [Dallas: A.H. Belo 1954]), 97, accessed through Portal to Texas History, https:// texashistory.unt.edu/.

5. "Tourism Well Dry: Town Still Crazy After All These Years," *Fort Worth Star-Telegram*, July 16, 1978, 18.

Chapter 1

6. U.S. Congress, *The Statutes at Large of the United States of America from May 1919– March 1921*, vol. 41 (Washington, D.C.: U.S. Government Printing Office, 1921), 759–812, http://home.hiwaay.net/~becraft/41Stats653.pdf.

7. There are conflicting dates concerning the original Guard interest in the Mineral Wells area. Many websites and secondary sources use the date of 1921 or 1925. Winnie Fiedler, in her thesis, *A History of Mineral Wells, Texas 1878–1953* (MA thesis, University of Texas, 1953; repr., Palo Pinto Historical Society, 2016), says that an infantry company was formed in early 1915 and was designated I Company of the Fourth Texas Infantry. In the *Scrapbook History of Mineral Wells and Palo Pinto County* (n.d. https:// texashistory.unt.edu/ark:/67531/metapth833750/), Bess Woodruff includes a news article that states, "Military operations first started in Mineral Wells in the early part of 1915 when an Infantry company was organized and designated as Company 'I,' Fourth Texas Infantry." The oldest newspaper documentation located online was in a newspaper clipping from the *Dallas Morning News* dated May 26, 1916, referring to Company I of the Guard from Mineral Wells. The caption of a photograph of the 112th Cavalry Band states that a unit of the Guard had been established on West Mountain in Mineral Wells in 1919. The *Pictorial History of Fort Wolters*, vol. 23, states, "1921- the 56th Cavalry Brigade of the Texas National Guard was organized and used the Rock Creek/Mineral Wells areas as field training areas." *The Historical and Pictorial Review: National Guard of the State of Texas 1940* (Baton Rouge, LA, https://texashistory.unt.edu/ark:/67531/metapth833790/) comments that land had been donated to the state for use as a permanent camp in 1926 but does not mention an earlier date. A mention of the Guard having an earlier settlement date in Mineral Wells can be found in the *Honey Grove Signal* from May 4, 1923. It describes eight carloads (freight

cars) of horses and equipment being received by the 112th Cavalry of Mineral Wells and states, "Stables for the horses have been built adjoining the armory." While an exact date is unclear, Fiedler cites a personal letter from a member of the 112th Cavalry, W.P. (Bill) Cameron, stating that "in early 1915" the Guard organized in Mineral Wells. Early 1915 is as close to a specific date as can be found.

8. "Texas Items," *Schulenburg (TX) Sticker*, June 13, 1924, 2, accessed through Portal to Texas History, https://texashistory.unt.edu/.

9. Fiedler, *History of Mineral Wells*, 74.

10. "The Weatherford, Mineral Wells, Northwestern Railroad Depot in Mineral Wells," photograph, 1890(?), accessed through Portal to Texas History, https://texashistory.unt.edu/.

11. John Lumpkin, "Explore Vintage Highways on a Bankhead Highway Daytrip," *Texas Highways*, December 28, 2020, https://texashighways.com/travel-news/explore-vintage-texas-on-a-bankhead-highway-day-trip/.

12. Janet Mace Valenza, *Taking the Waters in Texas: Springs, Spas, and Fountains of Youth* (Austin: University of Texas Press, 2000), 8.

13. Ibid., 74.

14. Ibid., 39–40.

15. Ibid., 40. Valenza's population for Mineral Wells in 1900 is incorrect. The population was 2,048. See William Hunt, "Mineral Wells, TX," *Handbook of Texas Online*, last updated April 1, 1995, https://www.tshaonline.org/handbook/entries/mineral-wells-tx.

16. Valenza, *Taking the Waters*, 74.

17. Ibid., 76.

18. Hunt, "Mineral Wells, TX."

19. Gene Fowler, *Crazy Water: The Story of Mineral Wells and Other Texas Health Resorts* (Fort Worth: Texas Christian University Press, 1991), 51, 62; Woodruff, *Scrapbook History*.

20. Fiedler, *History of Mineral Wells*, 93.

21. Ibid.

22. Ibid., 122.

23. *Mineral Wells Index*, March 12, 1927, in *Mineral Wells Index*, "The Creation of Camp Wolters," March 25, 2012, 9. This was reprinted in the *Mineral Wells Index* in 2012 from the original story that was published in 1927.

24. Fiedler, *History of Mineral Wells*, 122.

25. Hans P.M.N. Gammel, *The Laws of Texas 1927*, vol. 25 (Austin: Gammel's Book Store, 1927), 487–88. Fiedler (*History of Mineral Wells*, 121) states that the camp location is approximately three miles

from downtown Mineral Wells. There is a conflict about the acreage offered. In his dissertation on the Guard, Harry Krenek finds that the actual acreage was a lease, not a property gift ("A History of the Texas National Guard Between World War I and World War II" [PhD diss., Texas Tech University, 1979], 49, ProQuest Dissertation and Theses). Krenek writes that "the Mineral Wells Chamber of Commerce paid for the cost of a ten-year lease on 120 acres and the cost of an easement on 1,600 acres" for the Guard use (see footnote 62). He cites the *Journal of the Adjutant General of Texas* (1927), 11. This makes sense because Wolters had turned down a previous offer from the city of Waco for "fifty acres for the camp, a ten-year lease on ninety-five more acres, forty acres for a target range, use of a large area for maneuvering…and light, water, and telephone service to the camp for free." Even though Wolters may had been influenced to take the Mineral Wells offer by his friend, it would stand to reason that the Mineral Wells offer should be as good, if not better, than the Waco offer. Krenek later states that "a fifty-acre tract of land two miles north of Mineral Wells was deeded to the State for use as a permanent training camp for the 56th Cavalry Brigade. The State was also given a ten-year lease on an additional 120 acres and an easement was provided on a 1,600-acre tract for use as a maneuver area." He acknowledges the fifty acres but still lists the additional leased lands as being part of the agreement. Whatever the entire offer was, Mineral Wells' deed of fifty acres was accepted and signed off by the governor, and it is the only part of the offer officially recorded.

26. Fiedler, *History of Mineral Wells*, 122.
27. Krenek, "History of the Texas National Guard," 49.
28. Ibid.
29. "Guardsmen at Mineral Wells," *Dallas Morning News*, July 10, 1927, 7.
30. "Governor and High Officials Review Parade," *Dallas Morning News*, July 23, 1927, 1.
31. Texas National Guard, *Historical and Pictorial Review: National Guard of the State of Texas, 1940* (Baton Rouge, LA, 1940), 429; Frank Lotto, *Fayette County: Her History and Her People* (Schulenberg, TX: Sticker Steam Press, 1902), 231–35, 298–300; David S. Walkup, "Wolters, Jacob Franklin," *Handbook of Texas Online*, last updated March 30, 2019, https://www.tshaonline.org/handbook/entries/wolters-jacob-franklin; Texas Military Forces Museum, "Hall of Honor: Jacob F. Wolters," http://www.texasmilitaryforcesmuseum.org/hallofhonor/wolters.htm. Brevet Major General Jacob Franklin Wolters, a lifelong

Texan, was an attorney, soldier, state legislator, author, political strategist, leader and "Father of the Present Texas Cavalry." Born on September 2, 1871, Wolters grew up in the town of Schulenburg, Texas; he was the oldest of seven children. Wolters joined the Texas National Guard on May 31, 1891, studied law at Add-Ran College (later Texas Christian University) and was admitted to the bar on May 20, 1892, in La Grange, Texas. In November 1892, he was elected Fayette County attorney. He participated in the Spanish American War, World War I and in multiple militia actions in Texas between 1919 and 1932. He wrote two books, *Dawson's Men and the Meir Expedition* in 1927 and *Martial Law and Its Administration* in 1930. In 1925, he chose a site close to Mineral Wells as the home for the Fifty-Sixth Cavalry, which he commanded. Camp Wolters was named in his honor. He retired from the Guard in 1934 and returned home to his family in Houston but continued working as legal counsel for the Texas Company (later Texaco) until his death at the age of sixty-four. He died on October 8, 1935.

32. Texas National Guard, *Historical and Pictorial Review*.

33. Civilian Conservation Corps Legacy, "CCC Camps Texas," http://www.ccclegacy.org/CCC_Camps_Texas.html.

34. Fiedler, *History of Mineral Wells*, 122–23. One of the rock buildings that was built during this time remains on the campus of the current Mineral Wells High School.

35. Krenek, "History of the Texas National Guard," 50.

36. Franklin Delano Roosevelt, Executive Order 8530 Calling Out the National Guard, online by Gerhard Peters and John T. Woolley, American Presidency Project, August 31, 1940, https://www.presidency.ucsb.edu/documents/executive-order-8530-calling-out-the-national-guard.

37. Mark Skinner Watson, *United States Army in World War II, Chief of Staff: Prewar Plans and Preparations* (Washington, D.C.: U.S. Government Printing Office, 1991), 183–237, https://history.army.mil/books/wwii/csppp/index.htm.

38. The Guard spent $300,000 annually for the summer training camp. Not all of this went into Mineral Wells coffers, but a great deal did. Camp Wolters was also used as a camp by the ROTC and various other groups throughout the year. Fiedler states that in 1927, these groups spent an estimated $175,000 with local merchants (*History of Mineral Wells*, 122).

Chapter 2

39. Christopher Tassava, "The American Economy During World War II," *Economic History Association*, EH.Net Encyclopedia, February 10, 2008, https://eh.net/encyclopedia/the-american-economy-during-world-war-ii/.

40. "House Passes Defense Fund," *Brownwood Bulletin*, January 12, 1940, 40, 74, 1, accessed through Portal to Texas History, https://texashistory.unt.edu/.

41. Franklin D. Roosevelt, State of the Union Address, January 6, 1940, https://teachingamericanhistory.org/document/state-of-the-union-address-128.

42. Franklin D. Roosevelt, Letter to Adolf Hitler Seeking Peace, online by Gerhard Peters and John T. Woolley, American Presidency Project, September 27, 1938, https://www.presidency.ucsb.edu/documents/letter-adolf-hitler-seeking-peace.

43. Adolf Hitler, "Letter to President Roosevelt on Invasion of Czechoslovakia," Jewish Virtual Library, September 27, 1938, https://www.jewishvirtuallibrary.org/adolf-hitler-letter-to-president-roosevelt-on-invasion-of-czechoslovakia-september-1938.

44. U.S. Department of State, Publication 1983, "Defense Measures of the United States 1940," in *Peace and War: United States Foreign Policy 1931–1941* (Washington, D.C.: U.S. Government Printing Office 1943), https://www.ibiblio.org/hyperwar/Dip/PaW/index.html.

45. Roosevelt, Executive Order 8530.

46. U.S. Department of State, Publication 1983, "Defense Measures of the United States 1940."

47. Selective Service Act, Public Law 76-783, https://govtrackus.s3.amazonaws.com/legislink/pdf/stat/54/STATUTE-54-Pg885a.pdf.

48. *Texas Almanac 1941–1942*, 93; Paul Ord, "National Health Resort Becomes Doubly Famous with Location of U.S. Army's Largest Infantry Replacement Center," in *U.S. Army Speedometer*, March 1, 1941, 21, 3, 10, 9, accessed through Portal to Texas History, https://texashistory.unt.edu/.

49. Fiedler, *History of Mineral Wells*, 96.

50. Ibid., 119.

51. Bob Hopkins, "A Brief History of the Baker Hotel," Texas Escapes, August 2002, http://www.texasescapes.com/TexasPanhandleTowns/MineralWellsTexas/BakerHotelGhosts3BakerHotelHistory.htm.

52. Ord, "National Health Resort," 6.

53. Ibid., 5.

54. Colonel Willie H. Casper, *Pictorial History of Fort Wolters*, vol. 3, *Primary Helicopter Center Facility*, "Detailed History of Fort Wolters," point 43, accessed through Portal to Texas History, https://texashistory.unt.edu/.

55. "Spa Citizens to Washington," *Palo Pinto County Star*, September 27, 1940, 3, Boyce Ditto Public Library.

56. U.S. Senate, *U.S. Memberships and Assignments*, Chairman of Standing Committees 1789–Present, 46, https://www.senate.gov/artandhistory/history/resources/pdf/CommitteeChairs.pdf.

57. Ord, "National Health Resort," 6.

58. Ibid., 7.

59. "18,000 Men May Train at Mineral Wells," *Palo Pinto County Star*, September 13, 1940, 5.

60. *Palo Pinto County Star*, September 13, 1940, 3.

61. Ord, "National Health Resort," 7.

62. Ibid., 8.

63. Ibid.

64. "Mineral Wells Has Acreage Ready for Training Camp," *Dallas Morning News*, October 6, 1940, 9.

65. David Minor, "Rock Creek, TX (Parker County)," *Handbook of Texas Online*, last updated September 1, 1995, https://www.tshaonline.org/handbook/entries/rock-creek-tx-parker-county.

66. "ROTC's Camp Dallas to Be Leased to Army," *Dallas Morning News*, November 13, 1940, 1.

67. Willie H. Casper Jr., *Pictorial History of Fort Wolters*, vol. 1, *Infantry Replacement Training Center*, point "B," 43, accessed through Portal to Texas History, https://texashistory.unt.edu/.

68. Ibid., 3:43.

69. "Mineral Wells to Get Big Army Camp," *Palo Pinto County Star*, October 18, 1940, 1.

70. *Palo Pinto County Star*, October 18, 1940, 6.

71. "Mineral Wells Looks Ahead to Boom Days," *Dallas Morning News*, November 2, 1940, 8; "Camp a Certainty in Mineral Wells," *Palo Pinto County Star*, November 1, 1940, 1.

72. "Commissioners' Court Designates Health District," *Palo Pinto County Star*, November 1, 1940, 1.

73. *Palo Pinto County Star*, November 1, 1940, 1.

74. "Appreciation Dinner Big Success," *Palo Pinto County Star*, November 8, 1940, 4.

75. *Palo Pinto County Star*, November 8, 1940, 3.

76. "Bus Permits to New Army Camps Asked," *Dallas Morning News*, November 13, 1940, 6.

77. "Real Estate Boom on in Mineral Wells," *Palo Pinto County Star*, November 15, 1940, 1.

78. Casper, *Pictorial History of Fort Wolters*, vol. 1:39.

79. "Cage Brothers Contractors for Big Camp," *Palo Pinto County Star*, November 15, 1940, 1.

80. *Palo Pinto County Star*, November 15, 1940, 1.

81. John Binford, "Construction of Camp Wolters One of Greatest Battles Against Time and the Elements," *U.S. Army Speedometer*, March 1, 1941, 21, 3, 10, accessed through Portal to Texas History, https://texashistory.unt.edu/.

82. "Three Shifts Working Day and Night at Camp Wolters," *Fort Worth Star Telegram*, December 4, 1940, 9.

83. *Texas Almanac 1941-1942*, 93.

84. Paul Ord, "Mineral Wells Secures Infantry Replacement Center," *U.S. Army Speedometer*, March 1, 1941, 21, 3, 5, accessed through Portal to Texas History, https://texashistory.unt.edu/.

85. "Cows Move Out as Army Boom Makes Barn a Rooming House," *Dallas Morning News*, November 16, 1940, 1.

86. "They're All Cooped Up, Literally, in This Town," *Dallas Morning News*, December 22, 1940.

87. Binford, "Construction of Camp Wolters," 13.

88. "Post Office Employees Rushed," *Palo Pinto County Star*, February 7, 1941, 1.

89. *Palo Pinto County Star*, February 7, 1941, 1.

90. Ord, "Mineral Wells Secures Infantry Replacement Center," 7.

91. "Star Dust Column," *Palo Pinto County Star*, January 17, 1941, 1.

92. *Palo Pinto County Star*, January 17, 1941, 1.

93. "Three Shifts Working Day and Night at Camp Wolters," *Fort Worth Star-Telegram*, December 4, 1940, 9.

94. "Lake Charles Hotel Burns," *Palo Pinto County Star*, December 13, 1940, 1.

95. "900 Nurses Wanted for Army Posts," *Dallas Morning News*, December 29, 1940, 6.

96. "Work Slowed Down at Big Camp," *Palo Pinto County Star*, December 20, 1940, 3.

97. "Untitled," *Palo Pinto County Star*, December 13, 1940, 5.

98. "Camp Wolters Gets First Cupid's Call," *Dallas Morning News*, December 21, 1940, 12. The *Dallas Morning News* (March 21, 1941, 15) erroneously announced the first Camp Wolters newlyweds as Lieutenant and Mrs. Roy Inman; however, they would marry in March in Mississippi.

99. "Star Dust Column," *Palo Pinto County Star*, February 7, 1941, 3.

100. Binford, "Construction of Camp Wolters," 13.

101. "Camp Wolters Is Half Ready for Trainees," *Dallas Morning News*, January 15, 1941, 4.

102. Robert French, "Average Number of Days with 0.01 Inch or More of Precipitation, Palo Pinto County 1920–1943," in *An Economic Survey of Palo Pinto County Prepared for the Texas and Pacific Railway Company* (Austin: University of Texas, 1948), 2.010201.

103. "Camp Wolters Is Half Ready for Trainees."

104. "Work Slows Down at Big Camp," *Palo Pinto County Star*, December 20, 1940, 3.

105. "Boom Town Days in Mineral Wells," *Palo Pinto County Star*, November 29, 1940, 1.

106. "Texas Next Draft Call Set in January," *Dallas Morning News*, December 10, 1940, 10.

107. "$1,000,000 Contract Let," *Palo Pinto County Star*, November 22, 1940, 5.

108. "Camp Wolters Wiring Under Way," *Palo Pinto County Star*, January 24, 1941, 1.

109. *Palo Pinto County Star*, January 24, 1941, 3.

110. "Star Dust Column," *Palo Pinto County Star*, January 24, 1941, 6.

111. *Palo Pinto County Star*, January 24, 1941, 5.

112. "Star Dust Column," *Palo Pinto County Star*, December 13, 1940, 1.

113. "Boom Town Days in Mineral Wells," *Palo Pinto County Star*, November 29, 1940, 1.

114. "Quartermaster Assumes Duties at Camp Wolters," *Dallas Morning News*, January 3, 1941, 9.

115. H. Cleveland Ford, "Cage Brothers & F.M. Reeves & Sons Complete Outstanding Construction Job at Camp Wolters," *U.S. Army Speedometer*, March 1, 1941, 21, 3, 18, accessed through Portal to Texas History, https://texashistory.unt.edu/.

116. Binford, "Construction of Camp Wolters," 13.

117. "Work Progressing at Big Army Camp," *Palo Pinto County Star*, December 6, 1940, 1.

118. Ford, "Cage Brothers," 18.

119. Binford, "Construction of Camp Wolters," 13, 14.

120. "Troops to Move into Camp Wolters Feb. 15," *Palo Pinto County Star*, January 24, 1941, 1.

121. Binford, "Construction of Camp Wolters," 15.

122. "First Troops Received by Camp Wolters," *Dallas Morning News*, March 12, 1941, 8.

123. "Facts About the U.S. Army Replacement Center Mineral Wells, Texas" bookmark, in author's possession; Binford, "Construction of Camp Wolters," 15.

124. Ford, "Cage Brothers," 18.

125. Ibid.

126. Ibid. A worker was knocked unconscious in February when a ditch caved in on him, but no permanent damage was done (*Palo Pinto County Star*, February 14, 1941, 1).

127. Ford, "Cage Brothers," 18.

128. "Banks, Stores Enjoy Brisk Camp Wolters Trade," *Dallas Morning News*, February 23, 1941, 14.

129. "Star Dust Column," *Palo Pinto County Star*, January 24, 1941, 1.

130. "Round-Clock Effort Rushes Camp Wolters," *Dallas Morning News*, January 25, 1941, 4.

131. "Camp Wolters Will Be Ready for Troops," *Palo Pinto County Star*, February 7, 1941, 5.

132. "News, Commander Leaves for Camp Wolters," *Dallas Morning News*, January 2, 1941, 7.

133. "Quartermaster Coming," *Dallas Morning News*, February 1, 1941, 2.

134. *Dallas Morning News*, February 1, 1941, 2.

135. "Alien Arrested During Texas Sabotage Hunt," *Dallas Morning News*, January 9, 1941, 1.

136. United Press, "Seize German with 'Fire' Sticks," *New York Times*, January 10, 1941, 21, ProQuest.com.

137. "Are There Fifth Columnists in Palo Pinto County?" *Palo Pinto County Star*, May 31, 1940, 1.

138. "Resolutions Adopted at Mass Meeting," *Palo Pinto County Star*, June 28, 1940, 3.

139. "German Wants to Stay in Jail," *Palo Pinto County Star*, January 24, 1941, 1.

140. *Palo Pinto County Star*, June 20, 1941, 3.

141. "Mineral Wells Woman Says She Was Kidnapped," *Palo Pinto County*, February 7, 1941, 2.

142. "Officers Probe Army Fire," *Borger Daily Herald*, February 23, 1941, 15, 79, 1; February 23, 1941, accessed through Portal to Texas History, https://texashistory.unt.edu/.

143. "Highway Patrol Joins Forces with Officers of Three Counties to Reduce Deaths on Mineral Wells Road," *Fort Worth Star Telegram*, January 28, 1941, 1.

144. Ibid.

145. "Traffic Over 80—A Big Problem," *Palo Pinto County Star*, February 21, 1941, 1.

146. "Making Faces at Lady Cost Man $14 Fine," *Palo Pinto County Star*, February 7, 1941, 1.

147. "Officers War on Death's Speedway," *Palo Pinto County Star*, February 7, 1941, 6.

148. "Highway Patrol Joins Forces with Officers of Three Counties to Reduce Deaths on Mineral Wells Road," *Fort Worth Star Telegram*, January 28, 1941, 1.

149. "Wolters Soldier Killed," *Dallas Morning News*, May 13, 1941, 4.

150. "Camp Wolters Give Town Big Circus Night," *Dallas Morning News*, February 23, 1941, 14.

151. "A Year's History in Mineral Wells," *Palo Pinto County Star*, November 21, 1941, 5.

152. *Palo Pinto County Star*, January 17, 1941, 2.

153. "Jail Too Full for More," *Palo Pinto County Star*, February 28, 1941, 1.

154. "15,833 Pints 'Flu' Medicine Sold in Month," *Palo Pinto County Star*, February 28, 1941, 1.

155. "Counterfeit Camp Checks Reach Banks," *Dallas Morning News*, March 1, 1941, 8.

156. "Check Forgers Held," *Palo Pinto County Star*, April 18, 1941, 2.

157. *Palo Pinto County Star*, July 25, 1941, 5.

158. "Mineral Wells Café Workers Strike," *Palo Pinto County Star*, February 21, 1941, 1.

159. "Camp Wolters Near Completion," *Palo Pinto County Star*, March 7, 1941, 4.

160. "Defense Adviser Due at Camp Wolters," *Dallas Morning News*, February 25, 1941, 9.

161. "Mexican Aid Pledge to U.S. Renewed," *Dallas Morning News*, March 8, 1941, 3.

162. *Dallas Morning News*, March 8, 1941, 3.

163. "Camp Wolters Nears Completion," *Palo Pinto County Star*, March 7, 1941, 1, 4.

164. "Major Who Scored Camp Wolters Record to Get New Project," *Dallas Morning News*, March 7, 1941, 8.

165. "Camp Builder Honored," *Dallas Morning News*, March 14, 1941, 17.

166. "Camp Wolters Turned Over to Government," *Palo Pinto County Star*, March 28, 1941, 1, 5.

167. "Camp Wolters Builders Given Gold Watches," *Dallas Morning News*, March 9, 1941, 7.

Chapter 3

168. "Research Starters: US Military by the Numbers," National WWII Museum of New Orleans, as of April 1945, https://www.nationalww2museum.org/students-teachers/student-resources/research-starters/research-starters-us-military-numbers.

169. Ibid.

170. The Military Yearbook Project, "Army Replacement Training Centers, 1940–1941," https://173.247.251.131/references/general-references/army-replacement-training-centers-1940-41.

171. "General Simpson Honored at Weatherford," *Dallas Morning News*, March 9, 1941, 6.

172. "Lesley J. McNair," Military Wikia.org, https://military.wikia.org/wiki/Lesley_J._McNair.

173. Robert R. Palmer and William R. Keast, "The Provision of Enlisted Replacements," in *U.S. Army in World War II, The Army Ground Forces, Procurement and Training of Ground Combat Troops* (Washington, D.C.: U.S. Government Printing Office, 1948), 171, https://archive.org/details/TheProcurementAndTrainingOfGroundCombatTroops/page/n11/mode/2up.

174. Ibid., 867.

175. Ibid., 872.

176. Ibid., 872.

177. "Camp Wolters Now Belongs to U.S. Army," *Dallas Morning News*, March 22, 1941, 12.

178. Leonard L. Lerwill, *The Personnel Replacement System in the U.S. Army* (Washington, D.C.: Government Printing Office, 1954), 254, https://history.army.mil/html/books/104/104-9/index.html.

179. "Camp Wolters Range Firing to Commence," *Dallas Morning News*, March 27, 1941, 2.

180. The length of the training cycles changed throughout the war.

181. "Mineral Wells Training Center Hoists Old Glory," *Fort Worth Star-Telegram*, March 24, 1941, 2.

182. *Fort Worth Star-Telegram*, March 24, 1941, 2.

183. "Selectee" is what they called the men arriving to camp, as they had been selected randomly. While at camp, the terms *selectee* and *trainee* were both used.

184. "First Troops Received by Camp Wolters," *Dallas Morning News*, March 11, 1941, 8.

185. The camp handbook was officially titled "Camp Wolters, Infantry Replacement Training Center, Mineral Wells, Texas," and was in pamphlet form. It will be referred to in the shorter form "camp handbook."

186. B.N. Harlow, "Training for Military Service," *Annals of the American Academy of Political Science*, March 1942, 47.

187. Ibid.

188. "Camp Wolters Turned Over to Government," *Palo Pinto County Star*, March 28, 1941, 5.

189. "Leases Signed for Land at Camp Wolters," *Palo Pinto County Star*, April 18, 1941, 1.

190. "Reception Centers at Texas Camps to Be Increased," *Dallas Morning News*, April 24, 1941, 2.

191. Lerwill, *Personnel Replacement System*, 229.

192. "Camp Wolters Sends Trainees by Batch to Permanent Camps," *Dallas Morning News*, June 20, 1941, 3.

193. Germany began its invasion of the Soviet Union on June 22, 1941. The German and Italian consulates were closed in the United States on December 11; the Japanese invaded French Indochina on July 28 and accused the United States of invading its territorial waters in Sukumo Bay on July 31.

194. Thomas H. Eliot, "Did We Almost Lose the Army?" *New York Times*, August 12, 1991, Section A, https://www.nytimes.com/1991/08/12/opinion/did-we-almost-lose-the-army.html. The vote for the extension was 203–202. The vote was taken August 12, 1941.

195. U.S. Congress, U.S. Code 1982 Edition, *Title 50: War and National Defense*, Appendix, Chapter 7: Service Extension Act of 1941, Sections 351–62, 229–30, https://www.loc.gov/item/uscode1982-019050a007/.

196. "Morale of Army Is Okayed by Commander of 15,000," *Dallas Morning News*, August 25, 1941, 4.

197. George C. Marshall, "Speech at Trinity College, June 15, 1941," https://www.marshallfoundation.org/articles-and-features/marshall-troops/.

198. Marshall was adamant about the role morale played in the army. However, when the African American soldiers arrived at camp, there were no recreational activities or Service Club ready for them.

199. "Camp Wolters Men Entertained at Denton," *Dallas Morning News*, July 1, 1941, 9; "USO Dance Committee Fears Unbalanced Budget," *Fort Worth Star-Telegram*, August 30, 1941, 9.

200. "Former Yank to Hurl for Soldiers Sunday," *Dallas Morning News*, April 5, 1942, 6.

201. "Chico's Bit for Uncle Sam," *Dallas Morning News*, June 21, 1941, 10.

202. "Judy Garland to Appear at Camp Wolters," *Mineral Wells Index*, January 22, 1942, reprint in *Mineral Wells Index*, January 22, 2017.

203. "Goldwyn Emphasizes Movie's Place in Maintaining Morale of GI Joe," *Camp Wolters Longhorn*, December 29, 1944, 1, Briscoe Center for American History.

204. Richard Scholl, "Early Life, Enlisting, and Freezing in Texas," Digital Collections of the National WWII Museum, 2015, 2:29 mark, https://www.ww2online.org/view/richard-scholl#early-life-enlisting-and-freezing-in-texas.

205. "Camp Wolters Officers Sent to Philippines," *Dallas Morning News*, September 27, 1941, 2.

206. Lerwill, *Personnel Replacement System*, 269.

207. Ibid., 275. A provisional unit is a group organized for a short time for a specific action or task.

208. Ibid., 292.

209. Ibid., 271.

210. Ibid., 270.

211. Ibid., 271.

212. Ibid., 272.

213. Ibid., 272.

214. "Cycles Change to 14 Weeks," *Camp Wolters Longhorn*, July 2, 1943, 2.

215. William R. Keast, "The Training of Enlisted Replacements," in *The Procurement and Training of Ground Combat Troops* (Washington, D.C.: Government Printing Office, 1991), 402, https://archive.org/details/TheProcurementAndTrainingOfGroundCombatTroops/page/n11/mode/2up.

216. "54th Battalion," *Camp Wolters Longhorn*, August 6, 1943, 3.

217. Keast, "Training of Enlisted Replacements," 405.

218. "House by House," *Camp Wolters Longhorn*, August 18, 1943, 2.

219. "17-Weeks Cycle Explained," *Camp Wolters Longhorn*, September 3, 1943, 2.

220. "Camp Wolters Gets 11-Ton Tanks to Aid in New Training Program," *Camp Wolters Longhorn*, July 9, 1943, 1.

221. "New Machine Gun Range Named After Wolterite," *Camp Wolters Longhorn*, September 8, 1944, 1; "Hell's Bottom Gets New Bayonet Trainer," *Camp Wolters Longhorn*, October 20, 1944, 1; "Camp Adds Newest Flame Thrower to List of Practical Training Aids," *Camp Wolters Longhorn*, October 20, 1944, 5.

222. Lerwill, *Personnel Replacement System*, 273. Army Specialized Training Programs were a way that enlisted men, under the age of twenty-one, who had completed basic training and met minimum requirements on an army test, could continue to go to college instead of joining the military at that time. If they failed at their college work, they immediately had to join an army unit.

223. "10,000 ASTP Graduates per Month Will Meet Vital Needs of Army," *Camp Wolters Longhorn*, February 11, 1944, 2.

224. Lerwill, *Personnel Replacement System*, 277.

225. "110,000 ASTP Men Reassigned," *Camp Wolters Longhorn*, February 25, 1944, 5.

226. Lerwill, *Personnel Replacement System*, 291–92.

227. "Air Forces to Return Cadets," *Camp Wolters Longhorn*, April 14, 1944, 3.

228. Ibid.

229. "WD Transfers 80,000 to AGF," *Camp Wolters Longhorn*, January 5, 1945, 2.

230. "IRTC's Wheel System of Training Offsets Shortage of GI Instructors," *Camp Wolters Longhorn*, February 2, 1945, 2.

231. "General Stillwell Arrives Here for Tour," *Camp Wolters Longhorn*, February 16, 1945, 1.

232. "Twelfth United States Army Group," Military Wikia.org, https://military.wikia.org/wiki/Twelfth_United_States_Army_Group.

233. Lerwill, *Personnel Replacement System*, 301.

234. "Troops Hear Speakers Stress Continued Effort," *Camp Wolters Longhorn*, May 11, 1945, 1.

235. Lerwill, *Personnel Replacement System*, 305.

236. Ibid.

237. "Camp Takes News of Surrender Quietly," *Camp Wolters Longhorn*, August 17, 1945, 1.

238. "Graded Civilians Due for Cut Here," *Camp Wolters Longhorn*, September 14, 1945, 1.

239. "Camp Will Remain Open Indefinitely; Large Reduction in Civilian Workers," *Camp Wolters Longhorn*, December 14, 1945, 1.

240. "IRTC Trainee Strength Tumbles to 6,229 Men," *Camp Wolters Longhorn*, November 23, 1945, 1.

241. "Swan Song of Reporter Who Covered Them All," *Camp Wolters Longhorn*, December 28, 1945, 1.

242. "Most Camp Wolters Declared Surplus," *Fort Worth Star-Telegram*, January 24, 1946, 3.

243. Edward E. Coing, "The Last Days of Camp Wolters," August 15, 1946, 2, accessed through Portal to Texas History, https://texashistory. unt.edu/.

244. William R. Keast, "Importance of the Replacement Problem," in AGF Study, No. 7: *Provision of Enlisted Replacements*, 1946, 1, https://history. army.mil/books/agf/AGF007/index.htm#Contents.

245. "Flag Goes Down at Camp Wolters but Hopes Held for Hospital There," *Fort Worth Star-Telegram*, August 16, 1945, 1; "Last Battalions to Complete Training Tomorrow," *Camp Wolters Longhorn*, December 28, 1945, 1.

246. "Wolters May Become Vet Rehabilitation Center," *Fort Worth Star-Telegram*, August 16, 1946, 10.

247. "Flag Goes Down at Camp Wolters but Hopes Held for Hospital There," *Fort Worth Star-Telegram*, August 16, 1945, 1.

248. "Last Battalions to Complete Training Tomorrow," *Camp Wolters Longhorn*, December 28, 1945, 1.

249. Willie Casper Jr., "Detailed History of Fort Wolters," *Pictorial History of Fort Wolters*, vol. 3, *Primary Helicopter Center Facility*, 43, accessed through Portal to Texas History, https://texashistory.unt.edu/.

250. Casper, "History of Camp Wolters, Texas," 33.

251. David Minor, "Fort Wolters," *Handbook of Texas Online*, last updated January 22, 2022, https://www.tshaonline.org/handbook/entries/fort-wolters.

252. Keith Robinson, "Fort Walters," PBase.com, accessed February 20, 2022, https://www.pbase.com/keith1959/fort_wolters; "History of Camp Walters and Fort Wolters—Mineral Wells, TX," Waymarking.com, accessed January 27, 2023, https://www.waymarking.com/waymarks/ WMYEBX_History_of_Camp_Wolters_and_Fort_Wolters_Mineral_ Wells_TX; "Old Camp Wolters" HMdb.org, accessed January 27, 2023, https://www.hmdb.org/m.asp?m=119159; Spring Sault, "Fort Wolters: Former Military Base Is a Treasure Trove for Urban Explorers," Texas Hill Country, July 22, 2019, https://texashillcountry.com/fort-wolters-former-military/.

253. Binford, "Construction of Camp Wolters," 13; "Leases Signed for Land at Camp Wolters," *Palo Pinto County Star*, April 18, 1941, 1; "Reception Centers at Texas Camps to Be Increased," *Dallas Morning News*, April 24, 1941, 2.
254. "Camp Wolters, Infantry Replacement Training Center, Mineral Wells, Texas, pamphlet (handbook), 1, accessed through Portal to Texas History, https://texashistory.unt.edu/; Casper, *Pictorial History of Fort Wolters*, 1:22 .
255. "Camp Wolters is considered the outstanding replacement center of the country," stated Major General Courtney Hughes, Chief of the Infantry, in *Dallas Morning News* on May 24, 1941, page 3; Paul Reed, "Parachute School," *World War II*, September 2005, 18-20, in author's collection.
256. Lerwill, *Personnel Replacement System*, 469.
257. Ibid., 477.
258. "And Then There Were Fifteen," *Weatherford Democrat*, May 30, 2016, 1, https://www.weatherforddemocrat.com/mineral-wells/and-then-there-were-15/article_fa78cf68-24f3-5528-b2bc-8f64c3997f02.html.
259. "A Memorial Day WWII Hero Is Winning New Glory," *Philadelphia Inquirer*, May 24, 1998, 1, Infoweb-Newsbank.com.

Chapter 4

260. Camp Wolters, *Infantry Replacement Training Center, Mineral Wells, Texas*, pamphlet (handbook), 6, accessed through Portal to Texas History, https://texashistory.unt.edu/. The government used the term *colored* for African Americans, while the newspapers used the term *Negro* or *Negroes*. The author will use African American when not directly quoting.
261. A few words need to be said about the sources that are used in this chapter. Very few sources could be found on all three groups. Little mention of the African American selectees and the German POWs appeared in the camp newspaper, the *Camp Wolters Longhorn*. From that source, it was almost like neither group existed. What little information about these two groups that was found came from local or regional newspapers, oral histories and a few secondary sources. The African American battalions did have their own camp newspaper, the *Bugle*, but no copies are known to exist. The camp newspaper announced that German POWs were to be located at camp, and it was accompanied by a brief article; that is practically all they mention of the German POWs. The camp newspaper did feature stories on the WAACs (WACs) once they arrived, but the content is very

limited. However, this is the only source we have for them. Despite the lack of material, it is still important that these groups be mentioned and remembered as a part of Wolters.

262. Ulysses Lee, *The Employment of Negro Troops* (Washington, D.C.: United States Printing Office, 1966), 74, https://history.army.mil/books/wwii/11-4/index.htm#contents.

263. Ibid., 349.

264. "World War II Army Mobilizing Training Camps," GlobalSecurity.org, https://www.globalsecurity.org/military/facility/camp-ww2.htm.

265. "South Protests Negro Troops," *Santa Maria (CA) Daily Times*, August 15, 1942, Newspapers.com.

266. "Selective Service and Training Act," *U.S. Code Title 50*, https://tile.loc.gov/storage-services/service/ll/uscode/uscode1940-00505/uscode1940-005050a003/uscode1940-005050a003.pdf.

267. "First Troops Received by Camp Wolters," *Dallas Morning News*, March 12, 1941, 8 (see picture 29).

268. "Camp Wolters Initiates Its New Technique," *Dallas Morning News*, March 14, 1941, 3. Fort Huachuca had been the home for African American soldiers since 1913, when the Buffalo Soldiers were stationed there. It would see over thirty thousand African American soldiers during World War II, see https://home.army.mil/huachuca/index.php/about/history.

269. "Facts About the U.S. Army Replacement Center, Mineral Wells, Texas," Mineral Wells Chamber of Commerce, bookmark, accessed through Portal to Texas History, https://texashistory.unt.edu/.

270. "Last Battalions to Complete Training Tomorrow," *Camp Wolters Longhorn*, December 28, 1945, 1.

271. Camp Wolters, *Infantry Replacement Training Center, Mineral Wells, Texas*, pamphlet (handbook), 3, accessed through Portal to Texas History, https://texashistory.unt.edu/.

272. Ibid.

273. "Tuskegee, Ala.," *Chicago Defender*, August 15, 1942, 6, ProQuest.

274. Camp Wolters, *Infantry Replacement Training Center, Mineral Wells, Texas*, pamphlet (handbook), 5, accessed through Portal to Texas History, https://texashistory.unt.edu/.

275. Camp Wolters, *Infantry Replacement Training Center, Mineral Wells, Texas*, pamphlet (handbook), 6, accessed through Portal to Texas History, https://texashistory.unt.edu/.

276. "Ex-Chicagoan Proves to be Henry J. Kaiser of Guinea," *Chicago Defender*, September 4, 1943, 3.

277. "Many Trainees Will Depart," *Fort Worth Star-Telegram*, June 30, 1941, 3.

278. "3,000 Trainees Go to Army Stations," *Dallas Morning News*, July 8, 1941, 5.

279. "Lieutenant Colonels Given Assignments," *Dallas Morning News*, May 27, 1941, 10.

280. *Palo Pinto County Star*, June 6, 1941, 1.

281. "Brigadier General George Macon Shuffer, Jr.," *On Point*, 16, 4, 17–20.

282. *Palo Pinto County Star*, July 4, 1941, 3.

283. "Medal Given for Rescue," *Camp Wolters Longhorn*, July 24, 1941, 1.

284. "Vernon J. Baker," Digital Collection of the National WWII Museum, https://www.ww2online.org/view/vernon-baker#segment-2.

285. Howard Cabiao, "Vernon Baker, 1919-20," Blackpast.org, https://www.blackpast.org/african-american-history/baker-vernon-1919-2010/.

286. "Editor Transferred," *Chicago Defender*, January 23, 1943, 10; "In the Service," *Chicago Defender*, May 29, 1943, 9; "Everyone Goes When the Wagon Comes," *Chicago Defender*, January 31, 1942, 13.

287. "Army Day Big Success," *Palo Pinto County Star*, April 11, 1941, 4.

288. *Palo Pinto County Star*, April 11, 1941, 4. There was not an African American newspaper in Mineral Wells.

289. "Camp Wolters Soldiers Won't Lack Recreation: Citizens of Mineral Wells to Open Center," *Dallas Morning News*, June 13, 1941, 9.

290. "Mineral Wells to Dedicate Two Community Buildings," *Fort Worth Star-Telegram*, March 15, 1942, 4. Mr. E.E. McMillan conducted the opening day ceremony for the African American recreation center.

291. "Two Recreation Centers in Mineral Wells Are Ready," *Fort Worth Star-Telegram*, March 12, 1942, 18.

292. "27 Jim Crow Units Tabbed for $254,000," *Chicago Defender*, July 5, 1941, 7. The size of the service club was based on the size of units at each camp that housed African American soldiers. Camp Wolters had 1,500 to 2,000 African American troops and received a small club (for 500 to 3000 soldiers). It had a library of five hundred volumes, a junior hostess and a kitchen for short-order cooks. It cost about $5,000.

293. "Camp Wolters Club," *Chicago Defender*, October 4, 1941, 24.

294. "Army of U.S. Will Form 17 New Jim-Crow Bands," *Chicago Defender*, August 16, 1941, 6. Thirteen of the bands were formed at Infantry Replacement Training Centers, and four others in regular regiments. They were organized like other army bands and had the usual twenty-eight pieces.

295. "Organize Camp Band," *Chicago Defender*, August 30, 1941, 9.

296. "Everybody Goes When the Wagon Comes," *Chicago Defender*, June 30, 1941, 12.

297. "Pvt. Floyd Ray's Army Musicians Score Hits," *Chicago Defender,* September 8, 1942, 23.
298. "Camp Wolters, Texas," *Chicago Defender,* August 29, 1942, 24.
299. "Negro USO Opened," *Dallas Morning News,* October 7, 1941, 5; "Negro Girls Will Go to Camp Wolters," *Fort Worth Star-Telegram,* October 18, 1941, 15.
300. "Social Calendar," *Chicago Defender,* May 8, 1943, 6.
301. "Bronze Queen to Be Crowned at Negro Day at Fair Monday," *Dallas Morning News,* October 11, 1941, 1.
302. "Present Drama at Camp," *Chicago Defender,* June 27, 1942, 17; "Entertain Wolters Soldiers at USO Club," *Chicago Defender,* June 27, 1942, 17.
303. "Camp Wolters, Texas," *Chicago Defender,* July 18, 1942, 8.
304. "Black Spiders Will Play Negro Soldiers," *Fort Worth Star Telegram,* August 7, 1941, 8.
305. "Negro Soldier Nine Will Play Wonders Tonight," *Dallas Morning News,* July 19, 1942, 8. The Dallas Negro League team was the Dallas Black Giants. The Fort Worth Negro team was the Fort Worth Wonders. Rebel Stadium is in Dallas and was where the Black Giants played. This must have been an error caused by newspaper staff.
306. "Monarchs Play Wolters Team Here Thursday," *Dallas Morning News,* April 18, 1943, 8.
307. "Defense Housing Unit Names Are Approved," *Dallas Morning News,* August 30, 1941, 2.
308. "Civilian Aide Lauds Camp Wolters, Tex.," *Chicago Defender,* July 12, 1941, 7.
309. Jerry Ness, "Oral Interview with William H. Hastie," January 5, 1972, https://www.trumanlibrary.gov/library/oral-histories/hastie#transcript.
310. "Negro Army Officer to Inspect Camp Wolters," *Fort Worth Star-Telegram,* June 9, 1942, 13.
311. "Soldier's Volunteer Acts Shows High Morale of New Forces," *Dallas Morning News,* October 22, 1941, 6.
312. "Star Dust Column," *Palo Pinto County Star,* October 9, 1941, 1.
313. "Camp Wolters, Tex.," *Chicago Defender,* January 23, 1942, 10. Each battalion commander selected one soldier each day to be his "orderly." The soldier had to be neat in appearance and have an authoritative bearing. It is uncertain if this practice had been started at the opening of the camp but had become ingrained by 1943. In January 1943, the "orderly" duty fell to Private Nicholas L. Gerren. Before serving in the army, he had been a renowned violinist from Kansas, was the first African American

in the University of Kansas Symphony Orchestra and had studied at the Moscow Conservatory of Music. He would go on to receive a doctorate in music at the University of Kansas. His papers were donated to the university on his death in 2002.

314. Robert T. Starks, "Reviewed Work: The Invisible Soldier: The Experience the Black Soldier, World War II," *Annals of the American Academy of Political and Social Science* 428 (November 1976), 62–63.

315. Mary Penick Motley, *The Invisible Soldier: The Experience of the Black Soldier, World War II* (Detroit: Wayne State University Press, 1987), 98.

316. "Camp Wolters, Texas," *Chicago Defender*, October 24, 1942, 9.

317. Harvard Sitkoff, "Racial Militancy and Interracial Violence in the Second World War," *Journal of American History*, December 1971, 58, 3, 671.

318. "Dallas 'Off Limits' for Negro Soldiers," *Decatur (IL) Daily Review*, January 4, 1943, 20, https://www.newspapers.com/image/84657792.

319. "Civilians Surround Police in Hall-Thomas Area; Provost Marshal Arrests Seventy After Disturbance," *Dallas Morning News*, January 4, 1943, 1.

320. "13 Negro Soldiers Face Possible Court-Martial," *Dallas Morning News*, January 5, 1943, 1.

321. Sitkoff, "Racial Militancy," 671.

322. Ibid., 667.

323. Lee, *Employment of Negro Troops*, 426.

324. Ibid.

325. Sitkoff, "Racial Militancy," 680.

326. "Wolters Will Train No More Negro Soldiers," *Fort Worth Star-Telegram*, October 5, 1943, 10.

327. "Colored GIs Vacate Camp," *Camp Wolters Longhorn*, October 8, 1943, 1.

328. "City of Mineral Wells Buys USO Building," *Fort Worth Star-Telegram*, March 20, 1946, 2.

329. "Literacy Schools Use Colored Rooms," *Camp Wolters Longhorn*, April 7, 1944, 4.

330. "All Colored Revue to Show in Camp," *Camp Wolters Longhorn*, May 26, 1944, 3. Even with the African American troops being gone, there still seems to be some African American soldiers left at the camp. There are a few references that indicate this; however, they do not give any indication as to what kind of jobs they had or what units they were attached to, except for the camp band. The *Camp Wolters Longhorn* article "The Easiest Job in the World Is Not That of Army Bandsman" (March 3, 1944, 5) states that there are three bands at camp, "the

219th is the Colored band, which when split into a dance orchestra plays the hottest music this side of Hades." The *Dallas Morning News* article "Soldier Is Killed, One Hurt by Bolt" (May 20, 1944, 10) states that two "Negro" soldiers were hurt. The *Camp Wolters Longhorn* article "Negro Soldiers Hold Open House at RC" (June 23, 1944, 3) states that the celebration was in honor of Emancipation Day in Texas, also known as Juneteenth. Visitors toured the new African American guesthouse, recreation hall and barracks and watched the movie *The Negro Soldier* in Theater Two.

331. Judith A. Bellafaire, *The Women's Army Corps: A Commemoration of World War II Service*, Center for Military History Publication 72-15, https://history.army.mil/brochures/WAC/WAC.HTM.

332. Ibid.

333. Ibid.

334. Ibid.

335. "The Soldier Is a Gal," *Camp Wolters Longhorn*, October 13, 1943, 5.

336. "First WACs to Arrive at Camp Miss Train, Take Freight Caboose," *Camp Wolters Longhorn*, July 24, 1943, 1; "Camp Wolters WACS Celebrate Third Anniversary of Corps," *Camp Wolters Longhorn*, May 11, 1945, 2. It is stated in the July 7, 1944 edition of the *Camp Wolters Longhorn* that the WAACs stayed at the Baker from June 13, 1943, to August 2, 1943. They then moved into quarters at the Reception Center and finally into their own quarters in January 1944 (*Camp Wolters Longhorn*, May 11, 1945, 2).

337. "Contract Awarded," *Dallas Morning News*, September 5, 1943, 4.

338. "Camp Wolters WACS Celebrate Third Anniversary of Corps," *Camp Wolters Longhorn*, May 11, 1945, 2.

339. "First WAACs to Arrive at Camp Miss Train, Take Freight Caboose," *Camp Wolters Longhorn*, June 24, 1943, 1.

340. "WAC News," *Camp Wolters Longhorn*, July 9, 1943, 5.

341. Ibid.

342. "First Officer Ruth Chamberlain, Has Assumed Command," *Camp Wolters Longhorn*, August 13, 1943, 4.

343. "WACs See Allied Movie," *Dallas Morning News*, August 17, 1943, 11.

344. "Pvt. Alpha J. Hull, WAC, Transportation Section, Keeps Her Eyes on the Ball," *Camp Wolters Longhorn*, August 27, 1943, 6.

345. "Confusion About WAC Titles Ends Officially Wednesday," *Dallas Morning News*, August 30, 1943, 1, 8.

346. "WACs Are Eligible for Life Insurance," *Camp Wolters Longhorn*, August 27, 1943, 3.

347. "Welcome WAC Hop Featured at USO," *Camp Wolters Longhorn*, September 3, 1943, 3.
348. "Sports Program Set for WACs," *Camp Wolters Longhorn*, September 24, 1943, 7.
349. "Wolters WAC Cagers, Lose Overtime Tilt," *Camp Wolters Longhorn*, February 18, 1944, 7; "The Soldier Is a Gal," *Camp Wolters Longhorn*, April 7, 1944, 5. This "Soldier Is a Gal" column states that the name of the WAC baseball team was the "Eager Beavers."
350. "Camp Wolters WAC swimming team," photograph, *Camp Wolters Longhorn*, July 28, 1945, 1.
351. "U.S.-Born Japanese Girl Joins Air WAC," *Dallas Morning News*, November 7, 1943, 4.
352. "WACs Reject Japanese Girl," *Dallas Morning News*, November 8, 1943.
353. "WAC Detachment News," *Camp Wolters Longhorn*, January 7, 1944, 5; "WAC Detachment Has Grown from Eight Original Members to Strong Unit of 160," *Camp Wolters Longhorn*, March 17, 1944, 13.
354. "WACs Win Praise for Work Here," *Camp Wolters Longhorn*, March 17, 1944, 3.
355. "Camp Wolters Selected for District Headquarters in WAC Recruiting Drive," *Camp Wolters Longhorn*, May 12, 1944, 5.
356. "Mineral Wells Citizens Visit Wolters, WAC Detachment on Inspection Tour," *Camp Wolters Longhorn*, June 16, 1944, 5.
357. "Literacy School Discontinued," *Camp Wolters Longhorn*, August 11, 1944, 1.
358. "Camp Wolters Reception Center to Be Inactivated," *Fort Worth Star Telegram*, July 18, 1944, 7.
359. "Reception Unit Closing at Wolters," *Dallas Morning News*, July 18, 1944, 1.
360. Lee, *Employment of Negro Troops*, 261.
361. Ibid., 264. Please see Lee's full discussion for more on this topic.
362. "The Soldier Is a Gal," *Camp Wolters Longhorn*, August 11, 1944, 4.
363. Ibid.
364. "The Soldier Is a Gal," *Camp Wolters Longhorn*, August 18, 1943, 5.
365. "WACs Boast Own 'PXette,'" *Camp Wolters Longhorn*, November 3, 1944, 2.
366. "Camp Wolters WACs Celebrate Third Anniversary of Corps," *Camp Wolters Longhorn*, May 11, 1945, 2.
367. "Recruiting Halted for WAC and WAVE," *Camp Wolters Longhorn*, August 17, 1945, 3.

368. Bellafaire, *Women's Army Corps*.
369. Ruth Milkman, "Women's Labor Force Participation, by Marital Status 1890–1987," in *On Gender, Labor, and Inequality* (Chicago: University of Illinois Press, 2016), 263.
370. "The Soldier Is a Gal," *Camp Wolters Longhorn*, June 1, 1945, 5; "Don't Look Now, but…," *Camp Wolters Longhorn*, August 3, 1945, 6.
371. "Released WACs Have Job Rights," *Camp Wolters Longhorn*, August 31, 1945, 8; "WAC First Sergeant Leaves Detachment," *Camp Wolters Longhorn*, August 31, 1945, 1.
372. Bellafaire, *Women's Army Corps*.
373. George G. Lewis and John Mewha, *History of the Prisoners of War Utilization by the United States Army, 1776–1945* (Washington, D.C.: Center for Military History, 2004), 94, https://history.army.mil/html/books/104/104-11-1/cmhPub_104-11-1.pdf.
374. Ibid., 84.
375. In 1942, the Eighth Service Command included Arkansas, Louisiana, Oklahoma, Texas and New Mexico.
376. Lewis and Mewha, *History of the Prisoners of War*, 83.
377. Ibid.
378. Ibid., 104.
379. Ibid.
380. "German, Italian Prisoners to Labor at Army Posts," *Dallas Morning News*, October 13, 1943, 11.
381. "500 Prisoners of War Will Be Confined Here," *Camp Wolters Longhorn*, October 22, 1943, 1, 8.
382. Casper, "Timeline of Fort Wolters in Mineral Wells, Texas," in *Pictorial History of Fort Wolters*, 1:245.
383. "Course in Practical German Offered Wolters Personnel Working with POWs," *Camp Wolters Longhorn*, June 23, 1944, 1.
384. Colonel Willie H. Casper Jr. was a deputy commander at Fort Wolters during the Vietnam era. He took it on himself to write a history of the camp, starting with World War II and ending with Vietnam. He compiled multiple volumes, which he graciously allowed the public library at Mineral Wells to display and let patrons consult. In the section about prisoners of war, Colonel Casper said he had to rely on oral histories of longtime residents and writers from several of the local and regional newspapers, as the army ordered all records of individual camps destroyed "due to poor record keeping." He gave his history of Wolters to the Boyce Ditto Library in 2003. Most of the sources he mentions are no longer extant,

including local and regional newspapers. Those that are still around were checked for accuracy. Colonel Casper's history of the prisoners of war camp at Wolters is likely the most accurate account that exists.

385. Casper, *Pictorial History of Fort Wolters*, 1:88.

386. Ibid., 89.

387. An article in the *Denton Record Chronicle* dated January 1, 1946, states that there were 907 prisoners of war at Wolters at the end of 1945. This was unable to be verified.

388. Casper, *Pictorial History of Fort Wolters*, 89.

389. Ibid.

390. Ibid., 90.

391. Ibid., 89.

392. Ibid. Casper does not indicate what year this happened.

393. Ibid., 90.

394. "Civilian 'PWs' Draw Warning," *Camp Wolters Longhorn*, May 4, 1945, 3.

395. Casper, *Pictorial History of Fort Wolters*, 90.

396. Lewis and Mewha, *History of the Prisoners of War*, 77.

397. Casper, *Pictorial History of Fort Wolters*, 91.

398. "POW Labor Has Saved Army Over 19,000,000 Man Days," *Camp Wolters Longhorn*, May 26, 1944, 8.

399. Casper, *Pictorial History of Fort Wolters*, 90.

400. "POWs Fail to Show Up," *Fort Worth Star-Telegram*, July 12, 1944, 2.

401. Casper, *Pictorial History of Fort Wolters*, 90.

402. "Escaped German Prisoners Retaken," *Fort Worth Star-Telegram*, March 23, 1945, 25.

403. "Nazi POWs Taken Near Mineral Wells," *Fort Worth Star-Telegram*, March 23, 1945, 9.

404. "2 Missing PWs Returned Here," *Camp Wolters Longhorn*, March 23, 1945, 1.

405. "Capt. Erskine Replaces Major Johnson as Commander of Wolter PW Camp," *Camp Wolters Longhorn*, February 9, 1945, 4.

406. "Chaplain for PWs Assigned to Camp," *Camp Wolters Longhorn*, July 27, 1945, 5.

407. "Three PWs Killed in Explosion Here," *Camp Wolters Longhorn*, September 28, 1945, 1.

408. "3 POWs Killed in Camp Wolters Blast," *Fort Worth Star-Telegram*, September 22, 1945, 2.

409. Casper, *Pictorial History of Fort Wolters*, 91.

410. Ibid., 92.

411. This also implies that the latest date of arrival can be pushed back from June 23, 1944, to April 23, 1944.
412. Casper, *Pictorial History of Fort Wolters*, 95.
413. Ibid., 91.
414. "Prisoners of War in Texas Rapidly Being Repatriated," *Denton Record Chronicle*, January 1, 1946, 10, accessed April 29, 2021, https://www.newspapers.com/image/5192371.
415. Edward E. Coing, *The Last Days of Camp Wolters, 15 August 1946*, accessed through Portal to Texas History, https://texashistory.unt.edu/. Casper has it incorrectly listed as April 1945.
416. "Mineral Wells Man Holds on to Postcard from Former German POW Who Returned to Wolters," *Mineral Wells Index*, November 11, 2014, 1–2. Property of author.

Chapter 5

417. "Camp Wolters Soldiers Won't Lack Recreation; Citizens of Mineral Wells to Open Center," *Dallas Morning News*, June 13, 1941, 9.
418. "U.S.O. Plans New Centers in Mineral Wells," *Palo Pinto County Star*, October 24, 1941, 1.
419. *Palo Pinto County Star*, October 17, 1941, 2.
420. "Bids Let for Recreational Building," *Palo Pinto County Star*, October 24, 1941, 1.
421. "Question Marks Mean Girls Looking for Group Name," *Fort Worth Star-Telegram*, March 5, 1942, 9.
422. Camp Wolters, *Infantry Replacement Training Center, Mineral Wells, Texas*, pamphlet (handbook), 17, accessed through Portal to Texas History, https://texashistory.unt.edu/.
423. *Infantry Replacement Training Center, Mineral Wells, Texas*, pamphlet (handbook), 17.
424. "Mineral Wells to Open Non-Com Club Saturday," *Fort Worth Star-Telegram*, January 8, 1942, 9.
425. The Camp Wolters IRTC Handbook refers to this USO as "The Colored USO"; however, the *Dallas Morning News* article refers to the same building as the "Negro USO."
426. "Negro USO Opened," *Dallas Morning News*, October 7, 1941, 5.
427. "Camp Wolters Soldiers Won't Lack Recreation; Citizens of Mineral Wells to Open Center," *Dallas Morning News*, June 13, 1941, 9.

428. Ibid.

429. "Army Day a Big Success," *Palo Pinto County Star*, April 11, 1941, 4.

430. "Camp Wolters Soldiers Won't Lack Recreation; Citizens of Mineral Wells to Open Center," *Dallas Morning News*, June 13, 1941, 9.

431. "It's a Treat to Visit the Soldiers," *Fort Worth Star-Telegram*, February 22, 1942, 16.

432. "3,500 Attend New Year's Dance," *Camp Wolters Longhorn*, January 5, 1945, 5.

433. Ord, "National Health Resort," 8.

434. See chapter 2, which discusses the housing problem during the building of the camp.

435. "Palo Pinto May Benefit Further from Camp," *Palo Pinto County Star*, May 2, 1941, 2.

436. Camp Wolters, *Infantry Replacement Training Center, Mineral Wells, Texas*, pamphlet (handbook), 16–17, accessed through Portal to Texas History, https://texashistory.unt.edu/.

437. "AEF Program Gets Started at Wolters," *Dallas Morning News*, May 2, 1942, 4.

438. "Mineral Wells Café Workers Strike," *Palo Pinto County Star*, February 21, 1941, 1.

439. *Palo Pinto County Star*, May 9, 1941, 5.

440. "Construction Work Brisk at Weatherford," *Dallas Morning News*, April 16, 1941, 4.

441. "Mineral Wells to Get Defense Housing Units," *Dallas Morning News*, May 27, 1941, 7.

442. "Contract Awarded for Prefabricated Houses," *Dallas Morning News*, July 21, 1941, 8.

443. "Defense Housing Unit Names Are Approved," *Dallas Morning News*, August 30, 1941.

444. "Camp Wolters Opens Two Housing Projects," *Dallas Morning News*, November 30, 1941, 13.

445. "Mineral Wells Birthplace of Army's Rent 'Ceiling,'" *Fort Worth Star-Telegram*, January 29, 1942, 10.

446. "Mineral Wells Area Praised for Voluntary Control of Rentals," *Dallas Morning News*, August 22, 1941, 4.

447. "Towns Effect Own Controls Over Rentals," *Dallas Morning News*, August 29, 1942, 8.

448. In 1972, William T. Schmidt wrote a dissertation ("The Impact of the Camp Shelby Mobilization on Hattiesburg, Mississippi, 1940–1946" [PhD

diss., University of Southern Mississippi, 1972]) about Camp Shelby's impact on Hattiesburg, Mississippi, during 1940–46. In that dissertation, the author provides an answer to Mineral Wells' "voluntary" control. He says, "The village of Mineral Wells, Texas, immediately adjacent to Camp Wolters, an infantry training center larger than Camp Shelby, was one of the very few mobilization communities which succeeded in controlling rents without federal assistance. The author was informed by several prominent citizens who had served on the rent control committee that they formed a 'vigilante committee of twenty committee members which called in the night on landlords who refused to cooperate.' Today, the citizens of Mineral Wells consider their success in controlling the wartime inflation of rents as their proudest achievement during World War II" (44n78).

449. "Rents Advance in Three Cities," *Fort Worth Star-Telegram*, March 26, 1942, 9.
450. "Mineral Wells Birthplace of Army's Rent 'Ceiling,'" *Fort Worth Star-Telegram*, January 29, 1942, 10.
451. "7 Texas Areas Face Rent Cuts," *Fort Worth Star-Telegram*, June 24, 1942, 6.
452. "Rent Attorney Named for Camp Wolters Area," *Fort Worth Star-Telegram*, June 24, 1942, 4.
453. French, "Scholastic Population of Palo Pinto County Specified Years 1935–46," in *Economic Survey*, 4.1701, table 1.
454. "Supt. Ross Returns from Washington," *Palo Pinto County Star*, March 7, 1941, 1.
455. "Mineral Wells Schools to Be Improved," *Palo Pinto County Star*, November 7, 1941, 2.
456. "School Bonds Voted," *Dallas Morning News*, January 16, 1942, 2.
457. "Federal Funds OK'd for 2 Schools in Texas," *Dallas Morning News*, March 17, 1944, 2.
458. *Texas Almanac 1939–1940*, 111; *Texas Almanac 1945–1946*, 121.
459. French, "Per Capita Instructional Costs in Palo Pinto County Specified Years 1940–1946," in *Economic Survey*, 4.1701-02, table 5
460. "Contract Let for New Water System," *Palo Pinto County Star*, January 10, 1941, 1.
461. *Palo Pinto County Star*, September 26, 1941, 2; "Mineral Wells Water System to Be Enlarged," *Dallas Morning News*, October 28, 1941, 4.
462. "Mineral Wells Projects Set," *Fort Worth Star-Telegram*, February 8, 1942, 2.
463. "Filtration Plant Praised," *Fort Worth Star-Telegram*, April 17, 1944, 3.

464. "Water Restrictions Still the Camp Dry," *Camp Wolters Longhorn*, August 20, 1943, 1.

465. "Police Patrolling Highway to Town," *Camp Wolters Longhorn*, October 22, 1943, 2.

466. "State Police Curb Deaths on Camp Road," *Fort Worth Star-Telegram*, January 28, 1942, 13.

467. *Palo Pinto County Star*, October 10, 1941, 3.

468. "Youngster Fined $100 for Selling Intoxicated Liquors," *Pinto Palo County Star*, June 6, 1941, 1; *Pinto Palo County Star*, June 6, 1941, 1.

469. A letter dated October 21, 2021, from Palo Pinto County clerk Janette K. Green stated that they do not have statistical records for this time period but did provide statistical information for me on births, deaths and marriages from 1938 to 1945. Her cooperation is greatly appreciated. Phone calls to the district court personnel revealed that they had no information for this time that could be shared, and a letter to Palo Pinto County district clerk Jonna Banks went unanswered. Calls to the Record Department of the Mineral Wells Police Department and the Palo Pinto County Sheriff's Department proved unfruitful as well.

470. Mount Vernon.org, "Camp Followers," https://www.mountvernon. org/library/digitalhistory/digital-encyclopedia/article/camp-followers/.

471. Gus Blass, "Entering the Army," Segment Stub for 11353, Digital Collections of the National WWII Museum, accessed February 17, 2022, https://www.ww2online.org/view/gus-blass#entering-the-army.

472. "Texas Army Centers Solving Big Problem of Prostitution," *Dallas Morning News*, April 15, 1941, 10. *Vagrancy* was often the word used in polite society instead of prostitution.

473. Camp Wolters, *Infantry Replacement Training Center, Mineral Wells, Texas*, pamphlet (handbook), 13, accessed through Portal to Texas History, https://texashistory.unt.edu/.

474. "Questionable Women Ordered Out of Mineral Wells," *Palo Pinto County Star*, May 2, 1941, 1.

475. "Campaign on to Clean Up Mineral Wells," *Palo Pinto County Star*, October 10, 1942, 2.

476. *Palo Pinto County Star*, October 17, 1941, 3.

477. "12 Business Places Put 'Off-Limits,'" *Dallas Morning News*, October 20, 1941, 8.

478. "Camp Wolters Has Less Social Disease," *Fort Worth Star-Telegram*, July 11, 1942, 6.

479. Ibid.

480. "First 3 Cases Sent Center," *Fort Worth Star-Telegram*, April 27, 1944, 4. This does seem rather ironic as the Mineral Wells Venereal Clinic just had four women escape from the same facility in February. See *Fort Worth Star-Telegram*, February 13, 1944, 4.

481. "Success Is Reported for Rapid Treatment," *Fort-Worth Star-Telegram*, May 26, 1944, 14; "More Funds Allotted Mineral Wells Hospital," *Fort Worth Star-Telegram*, June 30, 1944, 4.

482. French, "Occurrence of Communicable Diseases, Palo Pinto County 1946-1947," in *Economic Survey*, 4.1710-11, table 15.

483. "Star Dust Column," *Palo Pinto County Star*, October 3, 1941, 1.

484. "Texas Legion Will Change Session Site," *Fort Worth Star-Telegram*, July 29, 1942, 13.

485. "County Banks in Fine Condition," *Palo Pinto County Star*, April 25, 1941, 1.

486. French, "Resources and Liabilities of Individual Banks in Palo Pinto County 1947," in *Economic Survey*, 4.1301, table 2.

487. "Mineral Wells to Have Big Airport," *Palo Pinto County Star*, August 1, 1941, 1.

488. "Contract on Airport Is Let," *Fort Worth Star-Telegram*, September 11, 1942, 15.

489. French, "Airport Facilities," in *Economic Survey*, 4.1003.

490. *Texas Almanac 1941–1942*, 493.

491. "Mineral Wells Steel Plant in Operation," *Fort Worth Star-Telegram*, June 12, 1943, 3; "Steel Casting Plant to Open at Mineral Wells," *Fort Worth Star-Telegram*, June 12, 1945, 13; "Hosiery Mill Secured by Palo Pinto Silk Industry," *Fort-Worth Star-Telegram*, August 6, 1945, 3.

492. *The Texas Almanac 1949–1950* (Dallas: A.H. Belo, 1941): 304, accessed through Portal to Texas History, https://texashistory.unt.edu/. In French's report, he states that there are thirty-one manufacturers in Palo Pinto County in 1947, but he does not list number of employees, salaries, etc. His source is the *Directory of Texas Manufacturers* for 1947, which the author is not able to locate.

493. *Texas Almanac 1941–1942*, 493; *Texas Almanac 1945–1946*, 489.

494. *Texas Almanac 1941–1942*, 493; *Texas Almanac 1945–1946*, 489.

495. This is the difference between dwelling units reported in 1940 and those reported for 1950 (*Texas Almanac 1952–53*, 97).

496. French, "Telephone Facilities in Mineral Wells," in *Economic Survey*, 4.1102-04.

497. *Texas Almanac 1941–1942*, 493; *Texas Almanac 1947–1948*, 507.

498. *Texas Almanac 1941–1942*, 493; *Texas Almanac 1945–1946*, 489. Many of the full-time staff bought homes in Mineral Wells and are counted as residents. The staff who lived on the base, as well as the trainees, were not considered residents.

499. Letter from Janette K. Green, Palo Pinto County clerk, October 21, 2021.

500. "Mineral Wells Pleasant 'Home in Texas' for Wives of Army Officers," *Fort Worth Star-Telegram*, January 31, 1943, 29.

501. Ibid.

INDEX

ABOUT THE AUTHOR

Stacy E. Croushorn has been the recipient of many generations of Camp/Fort Wolters stories. Her grandfather, father, mother and multiple other family members worked at Wolters for decades. She holds bachelor's degrees in psychology and social work from the University of North Texas and three master's degrees (in education, library science and history) from Tarleton State University, Texas Women's University and the University of Texas at Arlington; she is an educator and librarian, a former newspaper reporter and social worker and a lifelong storyteller.

www.ingramcontent.com/pod-product-compliance
Lightning Source LLC
Chambersburg PA
CBHW070348100426
42812CB00005B/1456